Conquering College Life
How to Be a
Winner at College

LAWRENCE GRAHAM, a senior at Princeton University, is a job and career counselor at Princeton Career Services. He has held several part-time and summer jobs, including student producer with NBC Studios, research assistant at the Ford Foundation, and aide for the Assistant to the President at the White House. His first books, *Ten Point Plan for College Acceptance* and *Jobs in the Real World,* brought him nationwide recognition in the *New York Times, People,* and *Good Housekeeping,* on the *Phil Donahue Show* and *Today Show,* and in other forms of national media. He has counseled and lectured to groups in schools, libraries, and community centers around the country on college and job-related matters.

Conquering College Life
How to Be a Winner at College

Lawrence Graham

WASHINGTON SQUARE PRESS
PUBLISHED BY POCKET BOOKS NEW YORK

A WASHINGTON SQUARE PRESS *Original* Publication

WSP

A Washington Square Press Publication of
POCKET BOOKS, a division of Simon & Schuster, Inc.
1230 Avenue of the Americas, New York, N.Y. 10020

ISBN: 0-671-46976-2

First Washington Square Press printing August, 1983

10 9 8 7 6 5 4 3 2 1

WASHINGTON SQUARE PRESS, WSP and colophon are
registered trademarks of Simon & Schuster, Inc.

Printed in the U.S.A.

To Betty,
One who has helped me
make sense of my world and myself.
To a new career.

Acknowledgments

Now that I have completed four successful years at Princeton University, I am confident that my strategies for college survival are foolproof. One very important thing that I learned during these four years was that no matter how hard you work, no matter how little you sleep, you'll never get anywhere without working with others. My family, friends, teachers, coworkers and classmates have all helped me in some way while I was gathering information or actually preparing the manuscript.

I want to thank my parents, Richard and Betty, who accepted all of those collect calls when I needed advice, support and an open ear. I am grateful to my Uncle Searcy who has been more than an uncle and a friend to me all my life, from elementary school to college. I would also like to thank my close friend and agent, Susan Zeckendorf, and my editor Marnie Hagmann, who saw the value in this book.

Others who helped me conquer my college years were my friends Adam Gottlieb and Jeremy Cohen; my Princeton roommates Lawrence Hamdan and Jordan Horvath whom I trust with my dark secrets; Nell Bassett at NBC Studios; Minnie

Reed at Princeton's Career Services Office; Sarah Taylor, Sharon Rowser, Marjorie Thomas, Bernard McDonald and Franklin Thomas at the Ford Foundation; and my writing teachers, John McPhee, William Howarth, Margaret Doody and Stephen Koch at Princeton. In addition, I want to thank Pamela Hut and Jody Seward for helping me with the manuscript, in spite of the short notice and their upcoming midterm exams.

And finally, I want to thank my brother, Richard, who was going through the rigors of dental school and giving me advice while I was learning the ropes at college.

Contents

4 CHOOSING YOUR COURSES

Advanced Placement • Mandatory Courses • Electives • Finding Out Course Requirements • Don't Judge a Course by Its Title • Researching Course Requirements • Why Locate the Easy Courses? • The Lower-Level Course • How to Locate the Easy Courses • Getting the Inside View on Courses • Talking to Students • Sampling the Courses • Talking to Professors Before Registration • Courses That Teach High-Paying Skills • Dealing with Your Dean and Adviser • Foreign Study

5 LECTURES, CLASSES, AND NOTE TAKING

The Importance of Lectures • The Importance of Classes • Are Lectures More Valuable than the Book? • Preparing for Classes and Lectures • Taking Notes in Lectures • Your Own "Shorthand" • When You Miss a Lecture • How to Ask Questions in a Lecture • Standing Out in Class Participation

6 QUIZZES, TESTS, EXAMS

Dealing with Exams Without the Anxiety • Situations That Create Exam Anxiety • Getting Copies of Exams • Knowing What to Study or Ignore • Getting the Most out of Your Notes • Creating Study Tricks for Any Subject • Forming Effective Study Groups • When to Study for Exams • Does Time of Day Matter When Studying? • Where to Study for Exams • How Older Students Can Help You • How to Cram When Necessary • Things to Do Right Before an Exam • Strategies in the Exam Room • Hints for Essay Exams • Multiple-Choice Exams • How to Deal with Bad Scores or Exam Failure

15 MONEY, MONEY, MONEY   150

Bank Accounts • Handling Financial Aid • Private
Scholarships • Scholarship Search Services • Special
Tips on Saving Money

16 SUMMER AND FULL-TIME JOBS   155

The College Placement Office • When to Look for Jobs
• How to Look for Jobs • On-Campus Recruiters • How
Teachers Can Help • Tips for Résumés • Tips for Cover
Letters • Tips for Interviews

17 GRADUATE SCHOOL AND CAREER DECISIONS   164

Graduate Schools • Selecting the Right School •
Finding Information on Graduate Schools • What to
Look for in a Graduate School • Entrance Exams •
Applying to Graduate Schools • Professional Schools •
Law Schools • Business Schools • Medical Schools
(and Other Health-Related Schools) • Schools of Social
Work • Fellowships • Getting Help From Alumni

1

LEAVING HOME
TO START
COLLEGE

As you read this guide, you'll find that there are many adjustments to make once you begin college. Although they may seem complicated at first, you'll see that these adjustments will come easily as you meet other students with the same worries and concerns. You will learn how to deal with roommates and new friends, as well as select teachers, courses, and your departmental major. As far as long-range goals are concerned, this book will tell you how to find campus jobs, summer jobs, and your first full-time job, as well as show you how to get into graduate or professional school. Pay special attention to the strategies on studying, writing papers, and handling stress. At the end of the book, you'll find the College Survival Calendar, an easy-to-understand guide that will help you conquer your college years, month by month.

To some students, college is seen as the great escape—from home, family, and high-school life. For others, it is the frightening experience of finally letting go of parents, home-cooked meals, and childhood friends. You may have had practice staying away from home by attending sleepaway camp, or you may never have left your family for any period of time.

No matter what type of home you're leaving, don't think that college has put a permanent seal on your past life. Just because you're beginning college in a different community or state doesn't mean an old life has ended. Yes, you will meet new people and make new friends, but by no means should you end old relationships. Look at college as a resource to add an ever-widening variety of personalities to your acquaintances.

Leaving Your Parents and Family

There are a lot of things to consider when you get ready to leave for college. One important point is the difference in freedom. You won't have your father there to tell you not to go to a party or your mother to warn you about finishing your research paper. Think how that freedom will allow you to enjoy yourself. Sounds great, doesn't it?

Well, now think about what else happens when you receive all this freedom. You end up with more *responsibility*. It may sound great to be away from your parents' nagging, but how will you get your schoolwork done? How will you keep your room clean? Of course you can do all these things without your parents threatening you, but it can be a challenge to accept all of this responsibility at one time.

Loneliness

Whether you're leaving a house where there are doting or loving parents or you are just leaving a good friend, you are bound to feel a bit lonely. Chapter 3 will tell you how to meet new friends, but what do you do about old acquaintances in the meantime?

Kelly was very close to her mother since her father had died. Since she had spent so much time with her mother during the last two years, she found it difficult to attend a college far away, in spite of her mother's insistence that she make friends. Although Kelly made new friends when school started, she spent the entire preceding summer worrying about being away from her mother. If you happen to be this close to a family member, remember that you can always visit on vacations and weekends, or telephone during the week. Don't avoid meeting other people in order to pout about people at home.

Parental Concerns and Roles

You may be happy to see your parents drive away after they drop you off at college, but don't think they are so happy to "let go" of a child after so many years. You should understand that parents react to the departure of a child in different ways, but they are all generally concerned that you be successful and happy. Some parents are the doting type that help you pack and offer to visit you every month and call you every other day. Then there are parents who worry. They will ask you questions like "Are you sure you can make it on your own?" "What are you going to do if you run out of soap, or money?" You may have the type of parents who cry that their little Jerry or Suzy is growing up. Just try to understand them.

These reactions are all expressions of concern. Your parents care about what happens to you, but they also know that they can no longer tell you how to organize your life.

When Earl began packing for college, he noticed a change in his parents. He saw that his father lost his temper easily and that his mother refused to let him borrow any money or use the car. Every time Earl turned on the television, his mother would tell him he watched it too much already. When he stayed out late, his parents would lecture him on the importance of studying when he had extra time. You can understand that, as September approached, Earl was glad to be leaving home. But you should also realize why his parents acted as they did. They tried to tighten up their rules and restrictions as a last-ditch attempt to teach Earl how to survive on his own. Since many parents don't know how to articulate their feelings, you'll have to do your best to read into their actions.

Danny was the youngest of three children and the last to leave home for college. Although his mother had been able to occupy her time when he was still in high school, she suddenly became bored after Danny left. She had no job and no more children at home to take care of. This is a common situation with nonworking mothers. Although this may sound chauvinistic, the mother's role is often a difficult one to adjust to when her children have left home for college. If this happens in your home, suggest that your mother join an activity that will take up her time or look for light, part-time employment or volunteer work. Treat your father in the same manner if he feels extremely lonely after you have left. You're not the only one who is worried about your college adventure. Your parents have to readjust to a new way of life, too.

Choosing Your Goals

All your life, you've probably heard that a college education is the key to success. Even if you don't become rich and famous, college will have helped you set your goals for the future. Many students are worried that they are not sure of what they want and therefore are unable to set their goals. This is what makes college so great. You don't have to know your goals before you get there—you select them as you continue your studies.

Even if you don't yet know which profession interests you, college will introduce you to a variety of possibilities through its alumni groups, career placement office, or special lectures. There is no reason to rush into your college career with the idea that you have to make all your decisions beforehand. This new knowledge will allow you to choose your goals realistically.

Significance of the College Record

Throughout this book, you'll learn how your college record will affect your future. Since your record includes not only your grades but also the extracurricular activities and jobs that you select during your four years, you want to make as few mistakes as possible. Your college record will be seen by admissions officers as well as employers if you apply for graduate school or jobs.

2
WHAT TO
BRING
WITH YOU

There are almost a million different things to bring with you when you go to college. Unless your college is around the corner from your house, you will have to spend time and thought in packing so that you won't have to have Mom and Dad mail sweaters, jackets, or typewriters to you.

The most important thing to do is to begin preparing for your trip to school at least a month or so in advance. You may have gotten ready for sleepaway camp in less than a week, but you probably didn't have to dress for more than one season of the year. When you arrive at college, you will need not only the right clothes but also certain books, appliances, furnishings, medicine, linen, and so forth. In this chapter, you will see what will be necessary for your time away from home.

Types of Clothing

Since school begins in the fall, it is reasonable to assume that you should bring all or most of your fall clothes with you. But before you pack anything, find out what type of climate exists in the area where your college is located. If you come from southern California and will be attending a college in New Hampshire, obviously you'll have to be prepared for weather much different from what you're used to. Some students prefer to wait until they arrive at college to buy the appropriate clothing, but this is extremely impractical. Not only will you find it difficult to locate stores if you don't have a car, but clothes shopping in college towns is time-consuming and very expensive. You should buy anything that you can in your hometown's lower-priced shops before you leave.

If you have never visited the college before and are concerned about clothing styles, as many students are, look in your copy of the college catalogue. It probably has pictures of students walking around the campus. Look at what they are wearing. Do they dress informally? Conservatively? If you are concerned about dressing as the other students do, and if you can afford to run out and buy an entirely new wardrobe, go ahead. As for the majority of us, we'll just have to bring what we have and add one or two shirts or sweaters that fit in with the surroundings.

Another thing to keep in mind is the length of time that will pass before you will be going home again. Some students go home during Thanksgiving and bring their winter clothes back with them when they return to school. If you aren't going home then or don't want the hassle of carrying clothes on your trip, you might as well pack your fall *and* winter clothes in September. Whatever you decide to do, it's a good idea to leave some articles of clothing at home, just in case you have to go home on an emergency and don't have time to pack. This way, you will at least have a change of clothes at home already.

When you begin packing, don't think you can get away with leaving your umbrella and boots at home. Even if your dorm is close to your classes and dining hall, you can still get wet. Another item that fits into this category is your basic canvas or nylon knapsack. It's not for camping—it's for your books. There is probably not a more practical way to carry your books. Slinging it over one shoulder allows you to have two hands free, and best of all, it is extremely durable.

Amount of Money

Even if your parents have paid for a meal contract and your room rent, you're going to need extra money for textbooks, school supplies, subscriptions to newspapers and magazines, and many other incidentals. How much should you bring? This all depends upon your spending habits and how much your parents and you can afford. The wisest thing is to bring a bank check or personal check that is large enough to open a bank account and enough cash to pay for a week of small incidentals. Incidentals can quickly add up to two hundred dollars or more.

If you don't have a meal contract awaiting you, figure out how much you will spend on groceries and utensils if you don't bring them from home. Add to this an approximation of your first phone bill. This all seems like a lot of money, but getting settled is always going to cost more than your day-by-day living. Also, remember that most college students have part-time jobs at school, so you can always reimburse your parents once you begin working.

Deciding What Roommates Should Bring

Sometime before you leave for school, you should write or telephone your roommate and ask what he or she can bring for the room. Since most schools will tell you in advance whether they furnish a desk, chair, or sofa, you will be able to figure out how much you and your roommate will have to ship to school or buy once you arrive. Most colleges supply each student with a bed (with a worn-out mattress), a chair, a desk, and a dresser for his or her clothes. This leaves you and your roommate responsible for rugs, window shades, hangers for your small closet, sofa, tables, desk or floor lamps, and shelves for your books, depending on the size of your room.

There is usually a way to divide these items between you and your roommate. When Bill called his roommate, Peter, he offered to bring his stereo and small refrigerator if Peter could bring a sofa, lounge chair, coffee table, floor lamp, and type-writer to share. One would hardly call this an even division of room furnishings, but Bill insisted that because his items were very expensive, he shouldn't have to bring so much. Peter argued that he would have to rent a truck in order to cart all of the furniture to school. You may find this amusing, but you'll be surprised to know that situations like this arise all the time. If there is absolutely too much for one or both roommates to bring, it's best to go without the expendable items (e.g., lounge chair, coffee table) or buy them used from a student at school.

You should also remember that there are certain things that just shouldn't be shared by roommates. These items include clocks, typewriters, and desk lamps. What happens when you have only one alarm clock and your roommate wants to wake up two hours before you do? He can always promise to reset the alarm, but it never happens. The hazard in sharing the same typewriter becomes evident when you both have a paper due at 9:00 A.M. tomorrow morning and neither has begun writing it yet. The case against sharing the same desk lamp is fairly obvious.

Another point to keep in mind when sharing things with your roommate is to avoid bringing expensive breakable items. Unless you know your roommate is responsible, don't expect him to treat your property as well as he would treat his own.

Necessary Appliances and Goods

Although most schools are beginning to outlaw toaster ovens and popcorn poppers in dormitory rooms, students are allowed to have a variety of other living appliances. Not that all of these items are necessary, but you may want to have some of the following:

iron	coffee maker
hair dryer	curling iron
clock-radio	phone-answering machine
vacuum cleaner	electric blanket
coffeepot	television

wall mirror
tape recorder
pencil sharpener
camera
water immersion heater
hot plate

refrigerator
stereo
electric curlers
humidifier
bathroom scales

You may find it useful in emergencies to include a tool kit, a first-aid kit, a flashlight, and a battery-operated smoke alarm.

Types of Books, Reference Materials

Although you will be buying your textbooks at the school store, you'll probably want to bring a good dictionary, a thesaurus, and any other volumes that you feel would be helpful. If you already know the required books for your courses, you may want to see if a nearby used-book store has them hidden away. You can save a lot of money by purchasing your notebooks and other desk materials during the end-of-the-summer sales at home. The school store will surely hike up its prices when the students arrive.

Personal Items

The list of personal items could go on forever when you think about the normal things that you use at home every day. Although you can buy most of them, it makes sense to bring as many as possible from home. You'll find that you may need these items at a time when you can't run to the store or borrow them from a friend.

medicine
sheets and pillowcases
pillow
scissors
laundry detergent
postage stamps
envelopes, paper

toiletries
plastic tableware
address book
office supplies
emergency supply of canned
    goods
records, tapes

sporting equipment	posters
identification	sleeping bag
travel suitcase or duffel bag	

Now, you may wonder how you're going to carry all this. Most students pack their clothes in duffel bags, suitcases, and a trunk. Heavier items like books can be put into crates. If you happen to have plastic milk crates in your attic, use them. Not only do they have handles for easy carrying, but they can also be stacked easily in your room to make extra shelving. Items like stereos and televisions should be put into sturdy boxes, preferably the ones they came in, so that they can be placed in storage when you go home on long vacations.

Of course there are other things that you can bring, such as filing cabinets, or inexpensive knickknacks to place around the room, or plants, but remember that all of this stuff has to be brought home at the end of the year. Only bring what you feel is necessary. You can always return for more during the next vacation.

Transportation

Whether you're going to a college in a major city or a small suburb, you'll probably be concerned about how you'll get around once you're there. Should you bring a bicycle, a car, or simply rely on public transportation?

Perhaps the most logical form of transportation is the bicycle. It is economical, easy to store, and can be used in the city as well as in rural areas. Unless you're prepared to be constantly vigilant, it's a good idea to bring an older, less expensive bicycle. Be sure to buy a lock and register the bike with the school and local police department.

If you can afford a car, make sure your school doesn't have rules against underclassmen driving on campus. While many rural and suburban schools will provide parking spaces for registered cars, they may not allow a freshman or sophomore to keep a car at school.

Once you've gotten permission, you'll find that there are

plenty of other headaches to consider. Not only will you attract a whole new crowd of "friends" who want to drive out to the mall or to a nearby college, but some will boldly ask to borrow it when they go on dates or short trips. Realize that you'll have to lay down rules for yourself and others. Don't waste all your study time cruising around town and don't waste all your money filling the gas tank. Save the car for the weekend and use it when a bus or train isn't convenient.

One of the most popular ways to get around while away at college is public transportation. If you are attending a small college where stores, classes and dining facilities are within walking distance, you probably won't even need a bicycle. If the campus is far away from services and stores, find out if there is a bus or subway route nearby. Except for using a car to get home at the end of the year, you can probably make do with the public transportation system.

3
ROOMMATES
AND FIRST
FRIENDS

When you start college, don't expect to have a room of your own as you may have at home. Not only will you have to share your bedroom, you'll also be sharing the bathroom as well as the living room (if you're lucky enough to get one). Although the common rooming arrangement for freshmen at most colleges is the *one-room double* (two people sleeping and studying in one large room), what is meant by a large double bedroom in many schools is about the size of a tight, one-car garage. Another common rooming arrangement is the *three-room quad* (four people living in a suite of two bedrooms and one living room for study and relaxing).

If you think this is close living, it can get a lot worse. There are such things as ten- and twelve-person suites (don't panic— you get two telephones). These suites—often labeled "the zoo"—are great if you like a busy social life, but they can make it almost impossible to study. Overall, the freshman-year rooming situation will be fair, and it's only just above fair at the prestigious schools.

Since close living is common at almost any college, the

roommate you get is going to make a tremendous difference in the matter. After you've been accepted by a college, the housing office will probably send you a form that asks you about dormitory and roommate preferences. As far as dormitory preference is concerned, request one that is center campus and that has other freshmen. The most important portion of the housing form, needless to say, is your roommate preference.

Your Roommate May Not Be Your Best Friend

In some schools you may have no choice of the roommate or roommates you will live with. The only thing you can be sure of in university housing is that your roommate will be of the same sex as you. Most colleges will ask you if there is a specific person with whom you would like to room. For instance, if you met someone at a summer orientation who is planning to attend the same college as you, you may request that person. But make sure that person also requests you, or otherwise you'll end up with someone else.

But what about the most common problem—when you don't know anyone else who's going to your school? This isn't as complicated as it seems, because the college will often provide you with a special form that allows you to indicate the type of roommate you would prefer. The form asks (1) if you smoke, (2) if you study in the room, (3) if you sleep with the window open, (4) if you like to play the stereo a lot, (5) if you would like to have a lot of roommates. The housing office takes your responses and then matches them with the responses of another student.

Although these questions won't guarantee that your roommate will end up being your best friend, they will at least guarantee that you have a few similar habits. And after all, you really wouldn't want a roommate who is a clone of your own character, sharing identical traits, backgrounds, and beliefs. Remember that dormitory life is meant to teach you to live with and learn about different types of people.

Choosy Suzy

If you are too selective about the roommate who's matched with you, you may end up like Suzy. Suzy was a typical college student—a moderate partygoer, she got good grades and liked to listen to her jazz records every now and then. She decided that the best roommate for her would be one who was the *absolutely perfect* student. In order to get this roommate, whoever she might be, Suzy made many stringent demands on the housing office. Like many students, Suzy thought she could have a perfect roommate by requesting a roommate who (1) didn't smoke, (2) didn't drink, (3) didn't listen to music, (4) didn't play sports, (5) didn't talk much, (6) didn't come from a large urban city, (7) didn't go to parties. . . . And the list went on.

Although Suzy had none of these traits herself, she felt that a roommate who did would make life easier. Believe it or not, there was another girl who requested most of these same characteristics. The girls were therefore placed together. The only difference between Suzy and her roommate was that the latter *really didn't do anything*. She was a real dud. (We'll talk more about the Dud later.) They ended up hating each other and Suzy wishing she had never looked for the model roommate. She should have been honest and looked for a student who would be more compatible with her own life-style.

Your High-School Chum

Every now and then, two best friends end up attending the same college. In many of these situations, the two students will decide to room together. There is no absolute rule on this, because every friendship is different. In most of these cases, however, there is one of three problems: (1) the two friends are so close that they never separate from each other to make new college friends; (2) the two high-school friends realize that they know everything there is to know about the other and are tired of each other's company; or (3) the two discover that they have entirely different living habits, even though they have similar social-life habits.

To remain safe, it is usually best to room with someone whom you don't already know. This way you can learn from each other and not tire so quickly of living together. Compatibility doesn't mean that you need to be the best of friends. The following list provides a group of questions to ask yourself when you are considering a new roommate. Since roommate selection happens every year at school, it's good to know what to look for in another person as well as in yourself when you *can choose* a roommate.

Your Own Roommate Questionnaire

1. *Does this roommate have either an overactive or an underactive social life?*
   Both of these people can be troublesome. The very active person may keep ridiculous hours, thus waking you at 3:00 A.M. or throwing parties every other night in your room. The underactive roommate may get disturbed when someone visits your room after 8:00 P.M.
2. *Is my roommate either incredibly sloppy or meticulously neat?*
   The disadvantages of having a sloppy roommate are obvious, but don't think the meticulously neat person is that much better. These fanatics will stop you from snacking in the room and will be forever vacuuming and searching for dust particles in every open space.
3. *Does the roommate have selfish tendencies?*
   A selfish roommate can lead to big problems when you have to divide the expenses for room furnishings or various room charges. Don't ever think you'll be able to borrow his typewriter when yours breaks down—but remember that the selfish roommate will always be borrowing and taking from you.

4. *Is the roommate a loyal and honest person?*
Everyone gets a little nosy now and then, but most of us can control our curiosity to a certain extent. Don't room with someone who is likely to rummage through your desk or steal change when he needs it. Although you can always lock your valuables in a trunk, who needs the hassle?
5. *Does my roommate accept responsibility?*
A roommate is someone who shares the responsibility of keeping room furnishings in shape, as well as taking your messages when you're out, and even helping you out when you're in a bind. It's better to room alone if you can't find someone who is responsible.
6. *Is this roommate a serious student?*
You don't have to room with an A-plus student, but it's good to live with someone who has a positive attitude about school. Not only will he motivate you to study, but he may also be able to teach you some things that he already knows when you need a tutor.

Roommate Types

No matter how careful you are at choosing a roommate, there is almost no way to be sure that you'll get someone you can handle. There are a few roommate types that, at first, seem like stereotypes on television—but, believe it or not, they really do exist in colleges. This guide will tell you what to expect from the Dud, the Conceited Bore, the Social Climber, the Jock, the Partier, the Cheapskate, and the Artsy-Fartsy Nature Freak.

The Dud

In most cases, the Dud hails from a town that was entirely forgotten during the last census count. He usually keeps to himself and is easy to please, but because the Dud is so lifeless, he is unable to understand why others are so active. He will complain when you play the stereo, when you come in late, when you receive calls after 9:00 P.M., and even when you eat in the room. Although he has no special interests, he studies hard, gets good grades, gets eight hours of sleep (even on Saturday nights), and enjoys using Friday evenings to wash his clothes and iron his plain white linen.

The Conceited Bore

The Conceited Bore usually comes from a city that was at one time a prestigious place to live, or a town that is on its way up but not quite there yet. What makes the Conceited Bore *so* boring is a deep-rooted feeling of insecurity. You can be sure that the Bore has dozens of photographs of her and her dog, her and her grandparents, her and her debutante escort, her and her uncle's potato farm, and her wearing her first high heels. She will start every sentence with "I" and end it with "me." Rest assured that she will tie her own experiences into anything, including this week's economics reading; the entire world is forced to reflect on her every action. The Conceited Bore always claims to be concerned with your problems but never has time to listen to them. Living with this person may be boring (because she is so predictable), but it will never be quiet because she is always talking about her plans, her dreams, her hopes, her past, and, naturally, *herself.*

The Social Climber

From the moment he first meets you, the Social Climber will be inspecting the quality of your clothes, asking what town you live in, what your parents do, and so forth. If your school provides a class directory with pictures of students, he will study it carefully and then select those people he must meet. And you can be certain that the Social Climber is not fooled when he asks you and you tell him that you are from a certain wealthy town when you're actually from some other town. He's already memorized which people are from the rich places, and he will boldly challenge you with a piercing stare and obnoxious questions. The Social Climber will take fencing lessons and then walk around campus with sword and mask to show all. He will never get an on-campus job, even though he needs the money. Although the Social Climber is never a true friend, he can always supply you with gossip on the powers that be.

The Jock

Of all the roommate types, Jocks unfairly receive the worst evaluations from people. They are frequently perceived as uncouth, clumsy people. Just because they spend 90 percent of their time jogging, playing football, lifting weights, or stretching their limbs doesn't mean they won't do well in their schoolwork. Believe it or not, the Jock often has an incredible amount of natural intelligence and rarely needs to study like the rest of us. One good thing about living with the Jock is that he is usually not the back-stabbing, competitive type when it comes to classwork; his aggression is taken out on the playing field.

The Partier

The Partier usually attends large universities in major cities like Los Angeles, Boston, or New York. The Partier sees herself as being on the innermost circle of the in crowd—she drives a metallic Firebird, uses Daddy's charge card, and believes that "bigger is better." When she isn't trying on new clothes, she's partying it up by herself or with friends. Usually seen with a drink in her hand, the Partier gossips mercilessly about her friends and gives phony three-minute laughs at the drop of a hat. Although she appears to be overconfident, the Partier is insecure and uses partying (getting drunk, stoned, etc.) to forget the problems that really plague her. Although the Partier can make life in the fast lane an exciting place to be, she will cause you to forget your priorities.

The Cheapskate

You'll probably know your roommate is the Cheapskate before you get to campus. He will write to you before school starts (a phone call costs too much) and ask you to give him a call sometime during the summer to discuss who will bring which room furnishings. When you call him, he'll say that you both will need a stereo, television, refrigerator, typewriter, and so on. When you ask him what he can bring, he will somehow beg off all responsibility. Not only is the Cheapskate stingy with his possessions, but he is also stingy with his time. He'll arrive on campus early to choose the best bed and desk. He will then quickly disappear, so you get to unload the car and all the furniture that you brought. The Cheapskate will magically reappear when the car is unloaded, the room swept, the shades hung, and the refrigerator in place and stocked with the food *you* paid for.

The Cheapskate not only borrows your money, your typing paper, and your roll-on deodorant *(Yuck!)*, but when he pays you back for anything, he gives you no more than he originally took. If he borrowed ninety-eight cents and pays you back with a dollar bill, he will always ask for the two cents change. This guy is a real nuisance.

The Artsy-Fartsy Nature Freak

In most cases, the Artsy-Fartsy will arrive at the campus two days after classes begin because she was on a nature walk through the crystal caverns of northern France and lost track of time. She will probably arrive at the dorm on an old bicycle with a guitar on her back. Inherently a selfish, narrow-minded person, the Artsy-Fartsy will immediately start shouting her liberal slogans and will rally for causes to disguise the fact that she hasn't the faintest idea what she wants. She calls herself a freethinker and yet criticizes anything that she doesn't understand. The Artsy-Fartsy will probably major in art history or Russian literature. She uses words like "cosmic," "organic," and "allegorical" to describe any situation. Since the Artsy-Fartsy sees herself as a champion of all who are discriminated against, keep your political and religious views to yourself.

Dealing with Difficult Roommates

Now that you have an idea of the types of roommates that exist at college, it's important to know how to deal with a problematic one who gives you constant worries. The first thing to remember is that many students who are beginning college have never shared a room before, so you have to give them a couple of weeks to become accustomed to your habits and your concerns.

But how do you know when that person is being inconsiderate? Is there ever a time to punch out your roommate to get him straight? How can you tell when it is time for *you* to move out? These are the questions that are bound to run through your mind.

After you have been living with a roommate for a couple of weeks, make a list of the living problems that you feel should be reconciled. Living problems can include being with a roommate who sets his alarm clock for 6:00 A.M. every morning but lets it ring until 6:30. A living problem can also mean a roommate who keeps you up at night because he can't stop talking in his sleep. Once you've made a list of these problems, decide which ones are the most serious. Since you want to bring these points to your roommate's attention as soon as possible, it's important to first focus on those that you feel strongly about.

But how do you decide which of your complaints are warranted and which are petty? This is a good question, because everyone has flaws. Since some of your habits may also annoy your roommate, you should know which grievances are important. The following is a small list of the living problems that you may confront. Check your own against the list and see if yours rank as a Very Reasonable Complaint, a Fairly Reasonable Complaint, or an Unreasonable Complaint.

Very Reasonable Complaint	*Fairly Reasonable Complaint*	*Unreasonable Complaint*
A roommate who:	A roommate who:	A roommate who:
• borrows without asking	• receives phone calls after midnight	• never plays the type of music that you like
• rummages through your desk	• sets his alarm clock for 6:00 AM on weekends	• is quiet and hardly speaks to you
• gets drunk during the week (in your room)	• has a large party in your room every weekend	• goes home to his parents' house every weekend
• forgets to lock the room when leaving	• plays the stereo when you are studying	

This list helps you put things into perspective when you are angry with your roommate. If your roommate plays music that you don't like, it can get very annoying, but remember that this is only personal taste. It's not his fault that you like another type of music. It's unreasonable for you to complain, because you can always ask him to use earphones, and because he is not infringing on your freedom—you can always leave the room. On the other hand, if your roommate always forgets to lock the door to your room, your complaint is very reasonable, because the result can mean theft or serious injury to you as well as him. This is a problem that *does* infringe on your freedom.

Once you know which problems you want to discuss with your roommate, do it at a time when you are calm. It doesn't pay to explode in anger, because he'll think you're being irrational and you may end up saying things that you don't mean. If speaking calmly doesn't work with your roommate, then it's time to go to your resident counselor or adviser.

Getting the Most from Your Resident Counselor

Most colleges provide new students with an upperclass counselor or adviser who lives in your dormitory. This person is paid to help you in your transition to college life. While you don't want to nag your counselor with small complaints, you should never be afraid to ask him or her to help you deal with a difficult roommate. These older and wiser students will not only serve as personal counselors for you, but they can also be mediators when you need help to solve a rooming problem.

Discuss your rooming concerns with the counselor, and ask him if he has any suggestions. Since these students have special training in these problem-solving areas as well as knowledge from their own personal experiences, they are usually extremely helpful. While you could always call Mom and Dad about your situation, the counselor is only two or three years older than you and can better deal with these peer problems.

In addition to solving roommate worries, a resident counselor can give you a good idea of the social and academic life at the school and information about other campus resources and facilities. Make sure that you attend any meetings that the counselor organizes for you. These meetings will not only teach you about the school, they will also allow you to meet other students who are also learning about college life.

During the first week of school, ask your counselor to give you a tour of the important areas on campus. Although the college may provide tour guides, these school-organized tours are generally designed for off-campus visitors who just want to see the handsome architecture and scenic gardens. The kind of tour you will want will include the library, the registrar's office, the career placement office, the infirmary, the laundry room, the dining hall, the bookstore, and so on. Always be polite to your counselor, and maybe ask him to join you for lunch a few times. This shows the counselor that you appreciate his time and enjoy his company.

Choosing an Older Student as a Mentor

It's always good to have a role model. If you grew up with a responsible older brother or sister, you were probably steered in the right direction by that person. Although there won't be a big brother or sister with you at college, you have others to help you learn the ropes. In addition to your resident counselor, you can also learn from a student who is a junior or senior. It may be someone who lives on your hall, someone who comes from your hometown, or even someone who is in the same course or extracurricular activity. Here is what Clever Claudia did when she was looking for a mentor during her first two weeks of school.

Clever Claudia

Claudia was beginning her freshman year at Tufts University. Although she was an outgoing person, she became impatient with her adviser's inability to introduce her to other students and deans. In order to learn about the places to go and the people to know on campus, Claudia started introducing herself to neighbors on her hallway. One person was a sophomore, two were juniors, and one was a senior. Since she was looking for an experienced student to learn from, she automatically eliminated the sophomore from consideration. One of the juniors was a boy on the football team and was an obvious knucklehead, so she eliminated him as well.

The two other students were a senior computer-science major and a junior history major. The senior would have been perfect, except for the fact that he knew very little about the social life on campus. Claudia concluded that, of the four, the junior history major would serve as the best mentor. Not only was the history major a fairly aggressive student like Claudia, but she was also a fairly pretty girl, so Claudia could meet lots of boys by being around her.

Although Claudia didn't find all the boyfriends she expected from her neighbor and friend, she did spend time with her and learned a lot about the school in just a few weeks. Never avoid becoming friends with an upperclassman simply because he isn't the same age as you. Not only will you enjoy the company, but you will also learn a lot from the past experiences of this older student.

How to Meet New People

No matter how eager you may be to meet new students and make new friends, it's difficult to introduce yourself to strangers and start a friendly conversation. One thing that you should always keep in mind when you begin college is that almost all of your classmates are as nervous as you are when they are trying to meet new people. Unless you are a social butterfly or the campus busybody, you probably dread walking up to a perfect stranger and introducing yourself. Since everyone wants to meet new people when they get to college, don't worry about which people you introduce yourself to; just speak to whomever you pass on campus.

One great idea is to use the Five-People-a-Day Plan. This is just a method to force yourself to meet at least five new people each day, and then remember their names and something special about them. If you give yourself a designated number of people to meet each day, it turns into a game that you'll enjoy. The best and easiest way to meet new people is in the dining hall. When you sit down at a table to eat lunch or dinner, don't look for an empty table. Look for a table where there are people whom you don't already know. Since you have a captive audience (they have to sit at least long enough to finish the meal), you can introduce yourself and start up a conversation.

Many people say that parties are a great place to meet people. In reality, parties can often be as unpromising as the theater as far as meeting new people goes. Many parties, like movies, take place in large, dark rooms where it is almost impossible to recognize anyone. In addition, people generally come in a group and leave in the same group. One way to meet other students is by doing your wash at a time when the laundry room is crowded. Another way is by joining an extra-curricular activity. Whether you join the campus newspaper or the tennis team or the radio station, you will quickly build a large group of friends who have some of the same interests as you.

Once you start running into more and more people, don't worry that your first questions will always be: Where are you from? Where did you go to high school? Where do you live on campus? What courses are you taking this semester? These questions seem mundane, but they serve a great purpose. They allow you to quickly find the characteristics that you and another person may have in common. Once you and a class-mate find something similar in your backgrounds, you will feel more comfortable with each other.

Dealing with Cliques

After the first couple of months of school, you'll begin to notice that classmates start to form small groups of friends with whom they spend most of their time. These cliques are very similar to the groups that form in high school, except that now the bonds between group or clique members are much stronger. To understand how these cliques work, look at how Karen finds her friends at school.

Karen was beginning her first semester at the University of Wisconsin. Although she didn't really like the girls on her hall, she realized that they were all the center of attention because of their outgoing personalities. Although Karen was a quiet person, she did want to have some friends. The six girls on the hall did everything together: they went to the movies together, they ate together, they walked to class together and even studied together. Karen decided that joining her six hallmates would promise lots of excitement. She started to go out with them constantly and really began to enjoy herself. But after a week, Karen realized that they never divided, and never invited others along with them. Not only did they all travel together, they all thought alike.

One evening, Karen's group was planning to see a movie that Karen didn't want to see. She said that they should go ahead to the theater without her because she didn't like violent movies. One of the girls said, "Oh, come along. We all want to see it." Karen refused politely, but the other girls got upset and said, "If you don't want to do what *we* want to do, then you don't have to do anything with us. We're a *group*." Karen then realized that it was time to move on and make some friends who weren't already trapped by group pressures.

Although it's easy to fall into a clique of friends, it's not always the best thing. Groups like this rarely allow individuality. You'll find yourself following a dominant leader like a sheep. Make an attempt to meet lots of different students who act and think like individuals. It will make college life much more enjoyable.

Housing Options

Since where you live on campus has a lot to do with the people you meet, now might be a good time to discuss such housing options as campus dormitories, off-campus apartments, fraternities, sororities and co-operatives. Although not every college offers such a variety of living arrangements, you may find yourself in the position of choosing between two or three forms of housing during your four years at school.

Campus Dormitories

The most common living arrangement at colleges is the traditional on-campus university-owned dormitory. Although there are still some schools that have single-sex dormitories, most colleges mix men and women by floor or even by room. If you are about to begin your freshman year, the housing office will explain their dormitory arrangements and ask you if you mind living on the same floor with another sex. If you *do* mind this, let them know. Many students think that it would be great to have men and women on the same floor, but they later find out that the old dormitories have only one bathroom per floor. And this means you've got to either create a co-ed bathroom or trek upstairs or downstairs to the closest bathroom for your sex.

Campus dormitories are generally favored by freshmen and sophomores because the buildings are conveniently situated to classrooms and dining halls. Another advantage to being on campus is that your classmates are in your building, and your landlord is the university.

At many large schools, campus dormitories are being turned into "mini-colleges" or "residential colleges" where a separate dining hall and small library are built for each dormitory complex. This is a great asset because it brings the students in the dorm closer together. Not only do you live in the same building, but you can also eat together. Too often, students at large universities get lost in the impersonal organization of one tremendous dining hall for the entire school to share. These residential colleges make campus living a little more intimate and relaxed.

Off-Campus Apartments

Another popular option that students have in most colleges is living off campus. If you are unable to pay for university housing and can find something cheaper, it may be a good idea to make different arrangements. Some students choose to live off campus because they want to have their own kitchen, or because they simply want more freedom or room than a dormitory can offer.

If you are a freshman, and the university can provide you with dormitory space, it may be a good idea to pass up the option of living off campus. Freshman year is the time when you should try to meet as many students as possible, and when you live off campus, you will be somewhat isolated and limited in the number of students you meet. Once you have formed more friendships, you may want to later get a group of friends and rent an off-campus apartment or house together.

When you finally decide to look for off-campus housing, try to find a place that is within walking distance of the library and your classes. Of course, if you're in a city school, you may be forced to live a bus or subway ride away, but in the suburbs, housing can usually be found nearer to the school.

Before you begin apartment hunting, stop by your school's housing office and ask for a list of suggested apartments and landlords. Too many students get ripped off by landlords who charge outrageous prices and provide horrendous service. You don't want to chase down a landlord when you discover there's no running water and no heat. Other good sources for locating responsible landlords are real estate brokers and older classmates. Check things out before you pay that first month's rent.

Fraternities and Sororities

If you attend a school that has an active program of fraternities and sororities, you may want to consider becoming a member of one. Although they are mostly known for their social aspects, these groups will generally provide housing as well as dining options for their members. Colleges that feature national fraternal groups will generally try to attract freshmen just before they begin "rushing," the process by which members are selected. Once you are accepted, you will probably begin living in your fraternity's house during sophomore year. For the next three years, you'll be living and eating in the same place with the same people.

Most fraternities and sororities employ a cook and one or two other workers to keep the facilities in order. Other activities and minor housing upkeep is performed by members and their officers.

Co-operatives

Another housing option that is offered on many university campuses is the co-op. This is a living arrangement in which the students all work together in keeping house, cooking, buying food and paying for repairs. When decisions are made about parties or purchases, the entire group is consulted. The greatest asset to these arrangements is that it provides students with a sense of community. It can also cut down on the time it takes to perform duties like fixing a meal and cleaning up after it.

4
CHOOSING
YOUR
COURSES

Remember in high school when your guidance counselor told you that you *had* to take four years of math, *had* to take four years of English, *had* to take four years of history, and *had* to take three years of science? Well, thank goodness for college. No longer will your entire course curriculum be decided for you. Now it's up to you to fulfill the basic requirements, design the best curriculum, and select the courses that fit into your program. While this all sounds so easy, it takes careful planning. The very first thing you should do when either selecting a college or entering a college is to read about the school's graduation requirements.

Most colleges and universities publish a free catalogue you can send for that lists the academic requirements for students. What you want to know is:

1. What is the basic number of credits or courses that one needs to graduate?
2. How many credits or courses do most students carry each semester?
3. How many credits is each course worth?

Some schools don't use the credit system. They simply say that a student must take 32 courses. (i.e., four courses for each semester), or they will say the student needs 116 credits to graduate. Credit and course requirements change from school to school, so it's important to find out early how many courses you should be taking during the year. After you've found out the academic-graduation requirements, it's time to find out which courses you are absolutely required to take and whether you qualify for advanced placement in any subject areas.

Advanced Placement

If you took advanced placement (AP) courses in high school, and did well on the AP exam, you may be able to receive college credit. Ask a dean or adviser whether you can get out of taking freshman biology because of your AP score. It's a waste of time to take entry-level courses if you have already demonstrated your knowledge on these tests. Some students even manage to graduate a year or six months early because they have gained extra credits through high school AP courses.

Mandatory Courses

In the past few years, many colleges have brought back the "core curriculum"—a fancy name for a group of courses that you have to take. While it seems like high school all over again, these mandatory courses are just lower-level requirements that will teach you the basics. Most colleges will require you to take one or two courses in the sciences, in English, in history or politics, in economics or math, in physical education, and frequently in a foreign language. So if you escaped taking Spanish or French in high school, don't think you're going to graduate from college without learning a foreign tongue.

Although you probably won't have to take all of these

mandatory courses during the first year in school, you may want to get them out of the way as soon as possible. Since these courses are on the most basic level, they can give you an idea of what you may want to concentrate in later. When you've made a list of all the mandatory courses, think about which ones you will take during the first couple of semesters. When that is decided, you can then start choosing your other courses—the courses that you *want* to take. Here is how Jeff selected his classes for the new semester.

Jeff was about to begin the second semester of his freshman year. When he began his college career, he was told that he had seven required courses to take (two English courses, two foreign-language courses, a biology course, an art course, and either a history or a political-science course). Since Jeff had already taken one of the English classes, one foreign-language class, and two elective courses during the first semester, he decided to next take the mandatory course that he dreaded the most—biology. Although he had never studied biology, Jeff was sure he would hate it. In addition to the biology course, he took the second language class and two more electives. Ironically, it took Jeff only one month to realize that the biology class was an exciting course. Not only did he sign up for two more biology courses for the third semester, but he eventually decided on biology as his major.

As you can see, mandatory courses can often introduce you to subjects that you never thought you would like. So when you find out what you have to take, don't consider it a restraint on your freedom; consider it a chance to expand your interests.

Electives

Now that you know how to handle mandatory courses, how do you choose your other courses? The best way to decide on your electives is by getting the course catalogue in the registrar's office. The next section of this chapter will give you details on using the catalogue.

Finding Out Course Requirements

When you choose your electives, you should not only take something that you will enjoy, but you should first find out what the course entails. Just because the name of the course is American History doesn't mean that it will include all of the years between the Pilgrims landing at Plymouth Rock and today; that "American History" seminar can mean just one ten-year period of American history, like 1820–30 or 1939–49. Too often students judge a course by its title and will check only the number of required papers and exams. Course requirements don't only include the exams, they include the number of topics to be studied as well as the depth at which topics are analyzed.

Don't Judge a Course by Its Title

When Flora was choosing her classes for the new semester, she looked through her college catalogue to get ideas for subjects that interested her. Although her catalogue did not explain what each course involved, Flora refused to spend time researching any further. She signed up for the Beginning Physics course because she had always wanted to learn something about physics. One week into classes, she was totally confused because she had never taken calculus—if she had asked someone she would have learned that a background in calculus was a prerequisite. The same thing happened when Flora took Macroeconomics I. Flora found out too late that there were two classes for Macroeconomics I—one class utilized complex mathematical formulas and the other did not. Flora ended up in the wrong class because she didn't know there was a difference.

Since Flora had always wanted to learn about Russian literature, she registered for Literature of Nineteenth-Century Russia. It was a shock to her when she got her first homework assignment to read a novel—in Russian. Flora had never studied the Russian language; she had just assumed that the literature was translated into English like her copy of *Crime and Punishment* at home. Flora ended up changing around her courses and missing a couple of important lectures because she didn't take the time to read about the topics covered in her courses. She foolishly judged each course by its name. Carol, on the other hand, was very careful about researching the requirements before she started her classes.

Researching Course Requirements

When Carol was about to register for a semester, she not only used her college catalogue to locate courses, but she also visited the department offices to get more specific information on the different courses that interested her. Most departments keep a notebook on file that has a one-page description of each course. Since Carol knew this, she carefully read through the descriptions, noting each course's level of difficulty. She had the following questions about each class:

- Is there heavy reading for the class?
- Is there a course prerequisite that I have not fulfilled?
- Does the class use a seminar or lecture format?
- How many papers (if any) and of what length will be assigned?
- Does the course require knowledge of a foreign language?
- Is the course one that only freshmen or only seniors take?
- Is this a course that covers a million different topics without really concentrating on one or two concepts?
- How often are exams given in the class?
- Does this topic interest me enough to take it seriously?
- Does my selection of courses for the semester allow lunch to fit in my schedule every day?
- Does this course provide the number of credits that I need?
- Does the course meet at a reasonable hour?

After Carol was satisfied with all of her courses, she registered for them with the assurance that she would find no surprises on the first day of class.

Why Locate the Easy Courses?

Every now and then, a student is in search of a class with a light work load. Although some courses are easy for some people and harder for others, there are a few courses that require less work for any student who takes them. These easy courses are often called *guts,* and they are often taken for the wrong reason. You might ask if there is any real reason for taking an easy course—there are plenty of good reasons. Gut courses are not just for people who only want to party their way through college (although this often happens); gut courses can also serve the serious student when his or her course load is already too heavy.

When Leo decided that he wanted to be an economics major, he registered for three economics courses in one semester. Since all three of them required a lot of problem sets and time for reading, he needed a fourth course that would not require too much effort. Leo therefore went searching for an easy class to balance his schedule.

Gut courses can also be used when you want to boost your grade point average. Alice was hoping to transfer from her college, but she wanted to raise her B-plus average. Although she was willing to work hard for her grades, she needed a course where her hard work would bring her an A. She registered for two easy courses and wound up with grades high enough to give her an A-minus average.

The Lower-Level Course

One of the most logical reasons for taking an easy course in a particular subject is to see if you like the department. Marty had always been fascinated by architecture, but he didn't know if he would enjoy studying a curriculum that would be so challenging. In his freshman year, he found the lowest-level course in the architecture department. Since it wasn't too challenging, he wasn't scared away from the field. The lower-level course was perfect for Marty because there were a lot of other freshmen in the class who also wanted to see if they liked architecture. He felt so comfortable in the class that he decided to take other courses in the department.

Now that you know *why* students should search for easy courses every now and then, let's see which strategies they use to find these courses.

How to Locate the Easy Courses

There are several strategies that you can use when looking for the course that will provide that "easy A" or a light work load. Although it is not true in every school, there are certain departments like visual arts and sociology that feature one or two easy introductory courses. While your college may not offer Basketweaving I, there are easy courses in your school that are disguised by their complicated names.

There are many courses with names like Modern Film Techniques and Geological Formations that might as well be called Tuesday Night at the Movies and Rocks for Jocks. Once you learn to read between the lines, by using sources other than the school catalogue, you won't be fooled by the sophisticated names of flimsy courses. If you want to know about an English course, visit the English department and ask for a detailed description of the particular course. If this is not available, then ask to look at some of the course's past exams that are kept on file. Although you probably won't get to keep the old exam, you'll at least get an idea of the number of topics covered in the class. By looking at the exam, you'll also see the course's level of difficulty.

Another way of finding out the difficulty of a class is to ask for the reading list. With this list of required books or articles, visit the bookstore or library and see if the reading is simple or challenging work. If you want to know even more, ask for the syllabus for the course. The syllabus will tell you what the professor expects from the students each week, as far as home reading and classroom activity are concerned. Even if you can't get hold of a new syllabus, ask for last year's—as long as a course is taught by the same professor, it rarely changes from year to year. If the syllabus says that you have only about fifty pages of light reading each week, you've found yourself a gut. If there is no reading, but just one short paper, you've found yourself an astrogut!

One thing to remember is not to be fooled by students who are always telling you how easy a course was for them. In many cases, the student is either lying and wants to impress you, or he just happens to be exceptionally talented in that subject. Another thing to consider is that some people perform better on exams than they do on research papers or in-class discussion.

Patty was a very tense person and therefore performed poorly in test-taking situations. To eliminate unnecessary pressure, she decided to look for courses that did not require more than one test during the semester. She was fortunate to find two courses that had no exams but did have final papers and in-class presentations. Her other two classes had take-home exams, so she wasn't under the type of pressure that she found in courses with in-class exams.

It's always important to find out how you will be graded in a course. Once you know this, you can then tell if the work is graded to your advantage. If you are a terrible writer, it's not going to improve your grades if you take courses that require all papers and no exams.

The final two things that you should determine when looking for an easy course are most important when you are considering science courses. Think of the grade curves on tests and the frequency of class and lab meetings. Science courses are notorious for having grading curves that will cause a certain percentage of students to fail the exam every time a test is administered. Science courses are also known to be accompanied by labs that meet for three or four hours twice a week. No matter how easy the concepts may be, this is a lot of time to spend on a course that is supposed to be lightening your load. With this in mind, remember that science labs should never be considered gut courses—they are time-consuming and unpredictable as far as grades are concerned.

When you start looking for an easy course, be realistic. Don't find yourself taking classes just for the high grade.

Although grades are important, a semester full of guts will only bore you to death and cause you to get turned off by college. Look for the easy course only when you want to lighten your work load or boost your grades a little.

Getting the Inside View on Courses

No matter what type of courses you're looking for, it's always important to get the inside story on a course. But even with all the college catalogues you read, you may never find out all the expectations of a course and its professor. If you really want to know what to expect, you need to start researching a course at least two to three weeks before you register for it. The most obvious method of getting the inside story on a course is by talking with fellow students the way Joe did.

Talking to Students

Joe knew that his classmates would be honest about the problems and benefits of the psychology course he was considering. Since Joe was only a sophomore, he was worried about the upper-level psychology class that he wanted to take. Although he asked his friends if they knew anyone who had taken the course, he found no one. Joe decided to visit the psychology department office and ask for the names of students who took the course last year. With this list, he started calling the students. He asked them if class participation was important, if the lectures were easy to understand, if the professor was a fair person, and several other questions.

If you decide to ask for a list of students who have taken the course you are investigating, don't be shy about calling the students. The worst they can do is tell you that they forgot what the course was like. If the department office does not save the names of students who took a course (although most do), get a list of seniors who are majoring in that department. It is likely that a senior has taken almost every important course that his department offers.

Sampling the Courses

In addition to speaking to classmates, you can find out about courses for yourself by sitting in on classes if your school has a shop-around period. Many colleges will give you a week or two to choose your classes by visiting lectures and seminars without registering for them. If your school doesn't have the shop-around option, find out if you can register for several extra courses and then drop those extra ones when you decide which you like best. It's always worth spending your time going to lots of classes and picking out the best ones. Listening to lectures will give you an idea of the course's content and will also allow you to see how many students are in the class.

Talking to Professors Before Registration

If your greatest fear is ending up in a course that features the scatterbrained or slave-driving professor, you may consider meeting the professor before classes start. Simply phone the professor or visit during office hours, and tell him or her that you would like to chat about the class for a few minutes. Since most professors would rather talk about their lectures than anything else in the world, you'll have no problem getting them into a long conversation. During your conversation, you'll be able to see if the professor is friendly or cold, open-minded or arrogant, as well as modest or pompous. Once you know what the professor is like, you'll feel more comfortable about the course itself.

All of these strategies will help you find the inside story on courses and professors. They will save you from worrying later and will eliminate any bad surprises when you arrive in class on the first day.

Courses That Teach High-Paying Skills

Since college is often the next step before reaching the world of employment, it's good to know which courses will give you extra skills that employers are looking for. Some of the most popular subjects that employers want students to have studied include computer science, economics, writing, business, a foreign language, and engineering.

Although it may be impossible to take courses in all of these fields, you can certainly learn a little about two or three of them. When Shari started her junior year, she decided that she would major in international affairs, and when she heard that most international-affairs graduates ended up in Spanish-speaking areas, she registered for Spanish I. No matter what field or occupation you choose, a writing course, or even a typing course, will aid you. Now that so many businesses are becoming computerized, even an introductory computer-science course will make your college transcript a little more appealing.

Dealing with Your Dean and Adviser

While college won't supply you with a guidance counselor who tells you how to choose classes, almost every college will provide you with an academic adviser or dean to aid you with academic questions. Don't be shy if you have questions—learn to use these people *before* you get into a problem. Meet with your adviser or dean each semester and ask for advice when selecting courses. While you should consider their opinions, never take every word they say as absolute truth, since they want you to work as hard as possible and will encourage you to register for the most challenging courses.

Most deans and advisers are happy to meet with their students, but too often students wait until they begin having problems with professors or grades before seeing them. In some colleges, the dean has the ability to provide you with a free tutor when you need one, but when you wait until you've got an F average, a tutor will help you only so much. Both your dean and your adviser can eventually serve as references when you begin job hunting or submitting applications to graduate school.

Foreign Study

The courses you take in college don't have to be limited to your own college; you should also look into taking courses at a university outside of the country. Many students, especially during a summer or during their junior year, spend one or two semesters at a foreign university.

Students generally choose to go during their junior year for several reasons:

1. Most students are fairly fluent in a foreign language by that time.
2. Juniors have declared a major course of study and know how to best organize their curriculum.
3. These students do not yet have the extra burdens of applying for full-time jobs and graduate schools that seniors have.

If you would like to study abroad, see an academic dean in your school who handles this area. The dean should have a list of programs at foreign universities as well as a list of American universities that have campuses on other continents. Before applying for a program, because many are competitive, make sure you can transfer all of the credits. Just because your school says you can go abroad does not necessarily mean you will get credit for your work. It's not worth studying abroad for six months and then later finding out that your college refuses to honor the courses you took. You may end up spending more money staying in college longer than the normal four years.

It's a good idea to begin making your plans for foreign study during the late fall of your sophomore year. Talk to your dean, read brochures, send away for applications and talk to older students who have been abroad. It can be a wonderful academic and cultural experience if you make your plans early and carefully.

5
LECTURES, CLASSES, AND NOTE TAKING

The first few weeks after your courses start meeting, you'll probably be very conscientious about your attendance, your note taking, and your class participation. As you join outside activities and fall behind in your schoolwork, however, those hour-long lectures will begin to look much less appealing. Whether you're a freshman or a senior at college, you're bound to ask yourself if you really need to attend classes or lectures in order to understand the material.

The Importance of Lectures

In this chapter, we'll be using the term *lecture* when referring to classes with more than thirty students. The traditional lecture is a situation where the professor usually stands at a podium or chalkboard and speaks, without interruption, to students in an auditorium or large room. The lecture is different from the *class* in that the latter usually features from five to thirty students and the professor may sit at a large table with the class. Later, we'll discuss some of the features of the class.

The lecture format of teaching is rather impersonal, since the lecturer is physically separated from the pupils and there is no dialogue between teacher and students. The purpose of a lecture is for the professor to deliver an organized presentation on a specific topic. Since lectures in many schools can comprise anywhere from thirty to a thousand students, it's no surprise that professor and student may never meet each other. Although one thousand classmates, a booming loudspeaker, and an echoing auditorium may seem forbidding, you'll quickly grow accustomed to it. You'll be glad to know that the largest lectures are usually reserved for the freshman introductory courses.

Now that you understand the format of the typical college lecture, let's consider its positive aspects. Lectures can be an extremely valuable source of education if you have a professor who spends a great deal of time preparing his presentation. One hidden benefit of lectures is that you can miss them as often as you want and never be penalized, since attendance isn't taken. One disadvantage to the typical lecture is that students are almost never allowed to ask questions. No matter how vague the professor's lecture happens to be, the student can only sit quietly and take notes.

The Importance of Classes

As mentioned earlier, the class is usually smaller than the lecture. There is more interaction between the professor and students in that there may be informal discussion or dialogue with questions and answers. Because of the personal nature of most classes, attendance and participation may play a part in your final grade. Whether the class sits at a large conference table or at desks in a classroom, the professor is bound to learn your name or recognize your face.

The advantages of the class format are quite obvious to the serious student. The class is where problems can be cleared up and new ideas debated. Not only can you grow closer to the professor in small classroom situations, but you will also feel more comfortable around fellow students. You'll learn the importance of knowing your professors as you begin a thesis or other forms of independent work or need recommendations for graduate schools or employers. Another advantage to classes is that they are usually more challenging and more exciting than rambling or tedious lectures.

There are, however, several important disadvantages to being in a small class situation. First of all, there is almost no way to come to a class without preparing in advance. Almost every student has been caught (at least once) without having studied the assignment. Since discussion is often very important in classes, you will be conspicuous when you sit in silence. You may get away with it in the first session by excusing it as shyness, but don't try it throughout the entire year or your class-participation grade may hurt you.

Another disadvantage to being in small classes is that there is rarely a way to miss class without having your absence count against you. Even if your professor doesn't take attendance, he may happen to remember that you rarely come. Since few students have the opportunity to attend colleges with small classes and close supervision, consider yourself rather fortunate if you find yourself in an intimate learning situation like this. You will find that many upper-level courses are taught on a classroom format.

Are Lectures More Valuable than the Book?

It was pointed out earlier that class attendance is often important for the sole reason that class participation is a part of your grade. But what about lectures? Since attendance isn't recorded and since you can't participate in discussion, do you really have to come? Can you simply read the text and learn all that's necessary to know? These questions are important if you simply must miss one or two lectures or are unable to sit through boring 9:00 A.M. lectures. Some professors assign certain pages in the main textbook and then merely discuss the exact same information in their lectures, without further explanation. Courses that only repeat the text reading can allow the student to get away without attending lectures, as long as he keeps up with the reading assignments.

If you aren't sure how important your lectures are, attend them for the first few meetings and keep up with the reading. Are you learning in the lectures something that you didn't learn from the reading? If your answer is no, then you can safely miss lectures without suffering too much. Whatever you do, be sure to get copies of the lecture outlines if your professor distributes them. These outlines are helpful for future reviewing. Even if you find the lectures dull and shallow, the professor may warn you that the exams will test you primarily on material covered in them. If this happens, follow his cue. Even if you keep up with the reading, you don't need any surprises when you take the final exam.

Although you have this advice on judging the value of lectures, don't miss them simply because you don't feel like getting up in the morning. While some teachers have designed amusing ways to keep you awake in lectures, others may come across as boring, in spite of the important information that they may present. If you have the smallest suspicion that a boring lecture may have some substance to it, go and listen.

Preparing for Classes and Lectures

It's always good to prepare for your lecture or class in advance. On the syllabus, you probably have assigned reading that relates to lecture topics or class discussions. While some people would rather wait for the end of the semester to complete the reading, you'll never understand the lecture unless you have some background information. As far as your classes are concerned, advance preparation is important if you want to impress the teacher with your participation. Preparing for class will probably include more than a mere skimming of the text. You should also develop some questions that relate to interesting points in the reading.

Taking Notes in Lectures

Note taking is an important skill for any student. It would be foolish to rely on your memory when you're moving from class to class every hour. The purpose of taking notes is to highlight the most important points of a professor's lecture. This may be complicated, since professors will rarely tell you, "O.K., students, write this down because it will appear on the test." Instead, the professor will simply present information and leave it to you to decide what is worth noting. If you happen to know shorthand, you may not have to worry about what to note and what not to note. Since the majority of us don't have shorthand skills, it is necessary to learn how to recognize only the most important material.

Randi worked extremely hard in her economics class. She was very concerned about understanding the lectures and reading material. When she arrived in the lecture hall, she took out her pen and began writing fiercely the minute that the professor opened his mouth. Because she was trying to write as much as she could, Randi never looked up from her notebook. When it came time to study for her midterm exam, she was shocked to find that she barely understood the notes she had taken.

When you take notes, you have to *look at* and *listen to* the professor as he speaks. When he makes a statement or interesting conclusion, you should rephrase it in your own words. Don't write paragraphs of information that don't make any sense to you. It's best to listen for a minute or two before trying to summarize a major point. When Randi took her notes, she failed to look at the professor to see if he made special gestures to emphasize certain points. A professor may raise his hand to draw your attention to a remark he is making. Or he may give you a special listing and number his points by holding up his fingers. There are all sorts of special signals that you miss when you keep your head buried in your notebook.

Some students foolishly rely on their classmates to cue them when to take notes in a lecture. How many times have you picked up your pen to write something down just because your friend wrote it down? This is not nearly as bad as refusing to take notes simply because no one else is. If the professor makes a point that you think is pertinent, make a note of it. Who cares if you're the only one writing? Here are some tips on taking notes:

- Use a spiral notebook. Loose-leaf notebooks are too large and cumbersome for small desktops.
- Use a ball-point pen that flows easily.
- Write legibly so that you'll understand the notes later.
- Use abbreviations as often as possible.
- Always look at the professor's hand signals.
- Don't write full sentences unless necessary.
- Use underlining and asterisks to highlight important points.
- Leave space in margins to add ideas or interpretations later.
- Always put the proper date on your lecture notes.

Your Own "Shorthand"

You may want to develop your own special symbols and abbreviations in your notes. Use arrows, squares, slashes, and so forth, to represent common ideas. Anything that you can do to make your job of taking notes easier, try it. You'll find that these simple shortcuts will even help prevent writing cramps when in class. If you limit the length of your notes, you also limit the amount of study time when you eventually use them to prepare for exams.

When You Miss a Lecture

If you must miss an important lecture, tell a classmate (who takes good notes) that you won't be there and that he or she should take "extra-clear" notes so that you can borrow them. Whenever possible, get a copy of the professor's lecture outline if he distributes one. Be careful of whose notes you copy from whenever the lecture is relatively important. Even though your friends may mean well, they may take sloppy notes. If you really don't trust them and can't find anyone else who is more responsible, give them a tape recorder and ask them to record the entire lecture for you. You can always count on the tape recorder to give you the accurate information.

How to Ask Questions in a Lecture

As discussed earlier, the lecture is usually reserved as the professor's own forum. But there may be situations where you feel you absolutely must speak up or ask questions. If you have an easygoing professor, you may be able to catch him just before he calls the lecture hall to order and ask one or two simple questions. Although it may be a little more difficult, you can do this just as the lecture ends and while restless classmates charge out of their seats. As far as interrupting the lecturer in the middle of his presentation is concerned, only try this if the lecture group is small and when the professor knows you well enough to answer you politely. Otherwise, don't try it!

Standing Out in Class Participation

There are all sorts of ways to make yourself become noticed and appreciated by your teacher when participating in class discussion. If your grade depends upon your participation, you should be concerned. Rarely will a professor allow you to sit in class and remain silent. If you try this, you're bound to get a grade that you'll regret.

Here are some sure methods to get noticed by your professor in class:

- Keep close eye contact with the professor.
- Make it obvious that you are writing what the teacher says.

- Try to be the first *and* the last student to make a comment during the class period.
- Never try to dominate the conversation in a rude manner.
- Act enthusiastic throughout the period.
- If you haven't done the reading, don't expose yourself by making foolish statements.
- Never allow a session to pass without making at least two remarks.
- Be sure to raise interesting questions for the teacher, but not so many that you make him or her feel uncomfortable.

6

QUIZZES,
TESTS,
EXAMS

No matter where you are going to college, there is almost no way to avoid taking exams. You've taken them in high school, so get ready to take more. Although the terms *quiz* and *test* are often used to denote a weekly or monthly exam, they all create the same anxiety in a great number of students.

Believe it or not, there are actually some students who don't mind taking exams because they enjoy working under pressure. For most of us, however, exams are a major cause of tension in school. Unfortunately, the tensions of exam anxiety are not limited to the thirty-minute or sixty-minute period in which you take the exam; the tension begins several days before, as you study, and then lingers on until you've gotten your score from the professor. Why is it that some students can handle this tension?

Dealing with Exams Without the Anxiety

Different people have different ways of looking at exams. The competitive person sees the exam as the only way to prove his knowledge. He constantly reminds himself that for every minute he wastes daydreaming or worrying, he will lose another potential point on the exam. The nervous student tells himself that he hates exams and hates the course. He is nervous because he is sure the teacher will use trick questions or score the test with a vengeance. This person will worry even more by convincing himself that everyone in the class is smarter than he is. The fun-loving person will look at each exam as a game that everyone has to play. He assumes that the test will challenge him in a way that will enable him to demonstrate all that he knows.

As you should have noticed, each of these three students has a different attitude about the exam he is facing. In many cases, it is not the difficulty of the exam itself that creates tension for you—it is instead the difficulty that you have *imagined*. Of course you can imagine that the teacher will use tricky questions or that she is out to get you, but none of these worries is going to help you before, during, or after the test.

The competitive person works hard, but for the wrong reasons. He is in for a big letdown because he thinks wasted time means lost points. He therefore worries about *not* wasting time; this is anxiety in itself. The nervous person is always thinking about the test, and that is good, but he sees it as an insurmountable wall—more anxiety. The fun-loving student, however, utilizes the positive idea of game competition to motivate himself. He realizes that a test, like a game, can never be the end of the world.

If you are the nervous or competitive type and find yourself a bundle of nerves before taking an exam, look at the following list of anxiety-causing situations. Since your attitude about the exam will greatly affect your ability to study, it's important to know how to avoid self-defeating behavior.

Situations That Create Exam Anxiety

You will create exam anxiety if you:

- Imagine that the teacher is your enemy.
- Think that your classmates are studying more than you.

- Tell yourself that you are not as smart as the other students.
- Assume that the exam will be made up entirely of trick questions.
- Ask other students how long they have prepared for the test.
- Imagine that the test is going to determine the graduate school you attend.
- Study with nervous people.
- Listen to people who constantly tell you how difficult the exam will be.
- Study when you are in a bad mood.
- Make bets with friends on how well you will score.

These are the situations that will hurt your chances of performing well on an exam. Make sure that you avoid them no matter how unimportant you might feel the test is.

Getting Copies of Exams

Although this strategy may appear to suggest illegal actions, it is completely legitimate. We're not talking about stealing a copy of the exam that you're about to take. We mean that you should try to locate a copy of last year's exam that was administered by the same professor. Many students are more comfortable preparing for a test when they can see how past exams were formulated. Since most professors don't radically alter the format of their exams from year to year, an exam from your economics course may be similar for three or four consecutive years. Here is what Althea did when preparing for her political-science midterm exam.

Althea was a sophomore in a political-science course that had been given at her school for the past five years. Since the midterm test was a week away and she had no idea of how difficult the exam would be, she decided to look for a copy of an exam that had been given during a previous semester. Naturally Althea could have spent hours studying every possible detail in her lecture notes and homework reading, but getting a copy of an old exam would help her choose what was most important to review. She told her older friends that she was looking for a copy of the test, and she found a senior who had not only taken the test three years earlier but had also saved his old midterm.

When Althea looked over the old midterm, she noticed that a different professor's name was on it. She found out that her teacher had not taught the course. Realizing that her professor would not use the exam format of another professor, Althea visited the political-science office and asked to see a more recent midterm—one that *her* professor had designed. She learned that her professor had started teaching the course two years ago, and she therefore looked for a one- or two-year-old midterm. She found a copy and studied the types of questions that were asked.

All of this seems like a lot of trouble, but Althea's perseverance came in handy when she began studying for the exam. She knew the style of questions; she found that there was an essay to be written. Quite often professors will not tell you the format of an exam or even give you a hint about the test's level of difficulty. It's dangerous to walk in blind to an exam, so check the departmental office or reserve desk in your library to see if old exams are saved for your perusal.

Knowing What to Study or Ignore

You can often find yourself studying *too much* material when exam time comes around. Many professors tell their students, "Study everything" or "You should be responsible for everything you've read this semester." Don't be fooled by this rhetoric. So much time can be wasted by studying the superficial information that you are given in lectures or in the course's main textbook. Even if you have plenty of time to study, it's ridiculous to spend it on things that the professor has no intention of using in exams. There are several ways to know what you should review and what you should ignore when looking through your assigned reading and your class notes.

In the Text

When studying from the course's main text (or texts), there are many different methods you can use. No matter what subjects you are studying, make sure you first glance at the pages or chapters that you were supposed to have read earlier. Although many students do their assigned reading well in advance of an exam, some students wait until the last minute to read the assigned material. No matter how much time you have, there are certain rules to follow when using a text to prepare for an exam.

First check to see if there are chapter *summaries* in your textbook. A summary is usually a one-page outline that appears at the end of the chapter. It emphasizes the major points that were raised in the reading and frequently provides brief, easy-to-understand examples.

Next, look for a *glossary of special terms* at the end of each chapter. If you are taking a course that uses a highly specialized vocabulary, a glossary will make reviewing of the text a lot easier and a lot faster. Finally, you can read the *subheadings* of all the sections of a chapter. This is similar to reading the headlines of a newspaper. If you have already read the chapter, a quick look over the subheadings will refresh your memory of its content. If this is the first time you've looked at the reading, the subheadings will help you organize your thoughts.

Getting the Most out of Your Notes

If you find yourself sitting in front of a pile of lecture notes just before an exam, don't feel discouraged. At the same time, don't think that because you wrote these notes a week ago, you will necessarily understand the material today. Taking the notes was only one step in the process of preparing for your exam. Now you have to actually study the notes.

A good way to work with your notes is to read through them and underline or highlight the significant points as you go. There are special pens and markers that you can use to highlight the important points in your notes. These markers will help you draw attention to significant points and help you ignore the extraneous information. One student in an Ivy League school was known to use four different-colored highlighter markers to signify the relative degrees of importance of certain points in his notes. The yellow marker was used for interesting facts. Green was used for important points. Pink was used to emphasize very important facts. Blue was used to highlight the absolutely most important facts.

On any one page, this student would have four different colors streaked across the lines of notes. Although this student thought this method was very helpful, not to mention decorative, it would take forever to even remember which colors were which. The best advice is to stick with one color and simply highlight those things that seem essential. Yellow highlighters are most popular because they are usually easier on the eyes. After you have highlighted the important points, you can refer back to your notes and quickly read those facts that are emphasized by their color.

Recopying Notes

Another easy way to review your notes is to force yourself to copy them over. It sounds crazy, but if you absolutely hate studying them over and over, make yourself copy them over, entirely. Although it is not the most thorough form of review, you will at least cause yourself to go over the ideas as you read them and then write them down again. This is a simple and painless method when you have used every other method of study or when you are too restless to study in silence.

Reading Notes Aloud

One more easy but helpful way of learning your material is by reading your notes aloud to yourself. When you read and hear the information out loud, it's almost like being in the lecture hall again. Not only will you notice certain points that you didn't pay attention to when you originally wrote them down, but you will also prevent yourself from glancing past words as so many people do when they read silently to themselves.

Creating Study Tricks for Any Subject

Everyone uses little games or mnemonic devices to memorize things they need to know. The reason why people do this is that it's easier to remember something when they have associated it with something that is different or fun. One of the simplest tricks that children are taught involves the memorization of the musical notation E, G, B, D, F. Some clever piano teacher realized that children wouldn't remember these letters as they stood alone, without any meaning attached to them, so the sentence "Every good boy deserves favor" was made up. As you can see, the first letter of each word corresponds to a note. Of course this may seem simpler than anything you may have to memorize for your chemistry or history exam, but it really isn't any different since you can use the same concept for any subject.

Barbara was preparing for a chemistry exam for which she had to learn the order of the first twenty chemicals on the periodic table of elements. Since each element has an official abbreviation like H for hydrogen, He for helium, Li for lithium, Be for beryllium, B for boron, C for carbon, N for nitrogen, and so on, she put all twenty abbreviations next to each other. Next, Barbara made up a story that used all twenty abbreviations at the beginning of each word in her story. It went like this: "*H*arry *He*lped *Li*onel *Be*come the *B*rightest *C*hemistry *N*erd . . ." Not only did Barbara have fun doing this, she had no problem remembering the chemicals for the rest of the year.

Even if you are unable to think up acronyms or study tricks for the more difficult material, at least use them for the simpler points that you have trouble keeping in order. This will allow you to concentrate on the more complex points in your study preparation. For instance, Stella had an American history exam in which she had to describe the administrations of several U.S. presidents. To eliminate the extra burden of recalling the order of the presidents, Stella used the first initial of the president's last name and created a story similar to the one Barbara had done for her chemistry exam. You can do this as much as you want when preparing for exams. The more hilarious you can make your study tricks, the easier they are to remember.

Forming Effective Study Groups

Even if your parents taught you to study in dead silence by locking you in your bedroom, don't assume that independent study is the best way to prepare for an exam. A popular and very successful method of test preparation by college students is the study-group method. This consists of getting a few of your classmates together and reviewing the material.

Paul was preparing for a history exam that was supposed to take place in a week. After reading through all of the material, he realized that it would take him three times as long to review it again all by himself. He searched around his class for some of the more intelligent students and found three others to create a study group. Paul insisted that they each read all the material before getting together. Each of the four classmates was to write up ten questions on a different section of the reading. When they got together, they quizzed each other and covered the material quickly.

Study groups can be formed with as many students as you like. Be realistic when you ask others to join you. Avoid asking people who are not disciplined enough to read the material in advance. After all, they won't be contributing anything if they are only absorbing the material that you've prepared. Also, don't use study groups as an excuse to socialize before exams; they can easily turn into parties if too many people participate. As long as you find responsible classmates to work with you, your studying can become more effective and more enjoyable.

When to Study for Exams

No matter what type of course you're taking, you will always be faced with the question of when to start preparing for a quiz or exam. Of course the perfect answer is that you should always be reviewing so you won't have to learn all the material the night before your test. But since you aren't perfect and since you don't have the time to review all of your subjects seven days a week, don't punish yourself. Even if you want to graduate first in your class, you won't want to study five hours every night of the semester.

The most practical way to figure out your study schedule is to look at the syllabuses your professors have provided. They should not only list your weekly reading and homework assignments, but they should also give the dates when tests will be administered. If they do not give dates of exams, ask your professors; this way you can give yourself enough time to prepare. The next piece of advice is never to allow yourself to fall behind in your reading by more than a week. If you lose a week or more, you'll find yourself walking into lectures without having the slightest idea of what's going on, and sooner or later you'll embarrass yourself in class if you're discovered by a skeptical professor.

If you have kept up with the reading and lectures, you can give yourself about three or four days to prepare for the average test. This allows you a chance to review everything in the first one or two days, and then ask the professor the next day any questions you might have. On the last day, you can make use of a study group to go over all the material one last time. This way, you can hear points about an issue that you had never considered during your early review of the material. For a weekly quiz, you can usually prepare in about one or two days. For midterms and finals, it is best to set aside a full weekend and three or four evenings to cover all of the material. Of course you can give yourself more or less time, depending on your grasp of the material and depending on the amount you are reading for the first time.

Two common worries that students have in regard to exams are surprise tests and last-minute cramming for tests. You should know that there are very few teachers who would ever consider giving a surprise exam in college. This is primarily a technique used by high-school teachers who want to teach the students to keep up with their studies. College professors don't have the time or the interest to teach you a lesson by scaring you. They save the scare until they give you your final grade for the course. The only types of surprise tests you might get are small five- or ten-minute quizzes in math or foreign-language courses. Although these may be graded, they rarely count much toward your final grade.

The second worry that students have is learning how to cram for a major exam when they only have one night to do it. Although your parents may tell you there is nothing so important that it should cause you to miss your sleep, you'll quickly find out that an exam is one of the exceptions to the rule. Later in this chapter, there is a detailed explanation of how to prepare during the eleventh hour. For now, try to avoid falling behind in those courses with frequent exams.

Does Time of Day Matter When Studying?

Some people like to study early in the morning, when their minds are fresh. Others like to study late at night, when everything is quiet. Still others prefer to study in the afternoon, before their minds get burned out. Each time of day has its benefits for different people. In college, as in high school, most students begin studying right after dinner and then continue into the night. This may not be the best time of day, though, if you are exhausted by 8:00 P.M.

Hector played on his school's tennis team, whose daily practice lasted from 4:00 P.M. to 6:30 P.M. When he was finished with dinner at 8:00 P.M. he was absolutely exhausted. He tried to study at night but found that he couldn't retain the material. After two weeks of ineffective studying, he tried waking up at 6:30 A.M. to do his work. Since he had always studied for two and one-half hours every day and didn't have a class until 10 A.M., he was able to do all of his reviewing in the morning after a refreshing night's sleep, a morning shower, and breakfast. Another benefit that Hector discovered from this early-morning study time was that his mind was totally clear of yesterday's worries.

It's a good idea to test your study time and see at what time of day you can learn more material. Don't decide on studying after dinner simply because your friends study then—try going to sleep a couple of hours earlier and studying before you go to classes. It may work.

Where to Study for Exams

Just as the time of day can help you retain what you study, so can the environment aid you when preparing for an exam. In this generation, many of us have grown up in front of the television or the stereo. We eat breakfast in front of the television, eat lunch in front of the television, and eat dinner in front of the television—why not do our homework in front of the television set? One reason why this won't work is that most college courses will require all of your attention when completing their assignments. This is why students who have noisy, stereo-playing roommates will either escape to a quiet library or insist that their roommates use earphones with the stereo. It may be a good idea to agree that the stereo will always be used with earphones between the hours of 7:30 P.M. and midnight so that no one is disturbed.

If you are fortunate enough to live in a single room, you may be able to stay there and avoid the library. The only drawback to staying in your room is that you can always be annoyed by the telephone, a noisy neighbor, or visitors who decide to drop in. But naturally, there are even some drawbacks to studying in the library. The library is often the main social scene for those students who do more chatting and whispering than anything else. The library also limits your freedom if you want to change the topic that you are studying. Unless you carried all of your textbooks to the library, you can't start working on another subject once you get bored with the first one.

Studying in the Exam Room

Here is a study trick that many students use to psychologically prepare themselves for the test-taking situation. They study for the exam in the same room where the exam is to later take place. Since every room is different, it's important to become comfortable in a room where you'll have to perform at your best. Studying in this room will also increase your ability to recall the information during the test, because people have the tendency to associate the learning of certain facts with certain places. This is why it is always best if your professor gives his or her exam in the same room where the weekly lecture was given.

How Older Students Can Help You

As you learned earlier, older students can aid you in your college career in a number of ways. One way older students can help you is by giving you advice on preparing for exams. They are likely to have study tips that are practical. If you are worried that a particular professor's exam will be very difficult, and you're unable to find a copy of an old exam, an older student who took the course earlier may be able to tell you that the test is one that requires little preparation.

How to Cram When Necessary

Even if you plan your time properly, it's almost impossible to avoid pulling an all-nighter at least once before you graduate from college. Sooner or later, you'll find yourself facing a major exam with only one day or, even worse, one night to prepare. There are certain rules you should know when cramming for an exam.

- If you're studying from a textbook, use the table of contents as a guide.
- Stock up with as much protein-rich food as you'll need to keep you going at night.
- Drink coffee or tea and study in a cold room to stay awake.
- Don't allow yourself to take naps, because you're bound to oversleep when you're exhausted.

- Borrow notes from friends who you know will understand the material.
- Don't spend time worrying about what you haven't studied.
- Read everything at least once.

Things to Do Right Before an Exam

There are some simple rules that will help you score better on exams. They include getting a good night's sleep the night before, among other things. Bernie had a final exam in two days. He made sure that he would get seven hours of sleep for the two nights preceding his 9:00 A.M. exam. Since the test was to last three hours with one ten-minute break, he thought it would be a good idea to bring a snack that would provide quick energy.

A candy bar, nuts, or raisins are good snacks when you have a long exam with a five- or ten-minute break. Avoid messy foods, such as potato chips or sticky caramel candies, that will only create the problem of having to wash up when there is not enough time. Also, avoid eating food in an exam unless you have a break. The opening of wrappers and the chewing of food will only ruin your concentration, annoy the other students, and take necessary time away from your work.

If, like Bernie, you have an early exam, don't wake up an hour before the test. Even if you normally get up at 8:00 A.M. for a 9:00 A.M. class, your mind has to be especially sharp for a test—get up at 6:30 or 7:00 instead and be sure to eat some breakfast, even if you normally don't. Morning exams are usually better since your mind is clear. Some cognitive psychologists suggest that a quick review of your material just before turning into bed at night will aid you immensely on a morning exam. This way, your mind will turn that information over and over until the next morning.

When you have an afternoon or evening exam, it may be a good idea to get away from other students an hour or so before the test time. Go for a short walk and try to clear your mind of everything that is unrelated to your course material. When you are finished with clearing your mind, get to the test room about twenty minutes before the exam begins. This will allow you to choose a seat that is away from a drafty window or a squeaky door. You can then sit quietly and look over your notes.

Strategies in the Exam Room

No matter how competitive your college is, you'll find dishonest students who will want to sit next to you or behind you in order to cheat off of your paper. To avoid this distraction, put yourself next to a wall or in a front row of the room. Few cheaters will be brave enough to sit at the front of a class.

Another nuisance is classmates who display their nervous tendencies in front of everyone. Everyone knows Last-Minute Lois, who is still studying fiercely when she walks into the exam room. Of course she can still learn something in the few minutes before the exam starts, but she'll scare you to death as she rushes nervously through a semester's worth of reading in less than ten minutes. Avoid sitting next to her.

Another person to stay away from is Joking Jerry, who never stops telling jokes and making wisecracks. Joking Jerry may be a riot at parties, but he will prevent you from taking the test seriously if you sit near him. Then there is Worried Wilma, who bites her nails feverishly and cries to everyone before and during the exam period that she is definitely going to fail. Worried Wilma will only put doubts in your own mind as you absorb her worries. The last person that you should look for is Stanley Showoff, who gets to the test early to let everyone know how much he has studied and how much they haven't. He usually starts off with a remark like "I bet nobody knows who was the original designer of the suspension bridge." His questions are always relevant to the course, but they are usually too difficult for anyone to recall the answer. The result is that everyone panics because they realize that there is something they *don't* know. Unless you have a great talent for ignoring people, get away from this loudmouth.

Hints for Essay Exams

Whenever you're taking an exam that requires you to write essays, it's a good idea to select the essay topic you know the most about. It rarely pays off to choose a difficult topic just to show the teacher your brave attempt; bravery doesn't earn you points on an exam. Once you've selected a topic, spend two or three minutes to sketch an outline for yourself. This may seem like a lot of time, but the minutes spent on organizing your ideas will help you to write quickly and concisely. Bring along a piece of scrap paper in case the teacher forgets to give you some. Another suggestion is *not* to copy your essay over in a neat form. Professors will rarely leave you enough time to copy an essay. If you start with an outline, you'll have fewer cross-outs and less need to make a neater draft of the essay.

Multiple-Choice Exams

There are also some tips to follow when you take a multiple-choice exam. You may think that a multiple-choice test is easy because the correct answers are at least given among your choices. This is actually the main problem with these tests—they are trying to trick you by mixing the correct answer with answers that are incredibly similar. One way to avoid being fooled by the answer choices is to read the question while answering it in your mind, then check to see if it's listed among the choices. If you look at the answers first, you'll have difficulty noticing the subtle differences between them.

How to Deal with Bad Scores or Exam Failure

Getting a bad score on a test is a part of college life. If you take grades too seriously, you can let them destroy you when you do poorly. For some of us, a D is a low grade; yet for others, a B plus is a low grade. It's good to set high goals, but if they are unattainable, you'll only frustrate yourself. When you get a low grade on a test, don't tear it up and start crying. Read through it to see what you did wrong. Don't ask other students how well they scored. This will only frustrate you if they received a better grade. Instead, look at your mistakes and arrange an appointment with your professor to go over your problems. Not only will the professor be impressed with your concern for your weaknesses, but he or she may give you a chance to improve your grade with an extra-credit project.

7

WRITING
PAPERS AND
ESSAYS

Since junior high school you've had to struggle through research papers and long writing assignments that kept you up late at night. Although these papers seemed like sheer drudgery, they taught you the valuable skill of writing. And it's probably no surprise that you'll be writing even more papers once you begin college. But isn't there an easier way of preparing term papers and other essays? There are several ways to choose a topic that you can handle and write a high-quality paper without spending hours at your desk or in the library. Just as Chapter 6 showed you the shortcuts of studying for exams, this chapter will show you the least exhausting methods for writing papers.

Although most courses require that you write only one or two papers, there are some courses that ask for three or four papers during the semester. As mentioned earlier, English, history, political science, and art history are popular paper-writing departments, whereas math, economics, and the sciences put more emphasis on problem sets and exams. Perhaps the most difficult papers to prepare are those that deal with philosophical issues. Although most philosophy papers are supposed to be relatively short, they are especially complex because they require careful argumentation when proving or disproving a point. Let's look at some of the general strategies to use when writing almost any type of paper.

Choosing the Right Topic for You

You can immediatley cut down on unnecessary labor by choosing a topic that you will enjoy working with. If your professor has given you a wide choice of topics to write about, it certainly doesn't make sense to choose one that will bore you. In order to write a good paper, you have to force yourself to fall in love with the subject. And who can fall in love with a topic like "The Economic Recovery of Underdeveloped Celtic-speaking Countries" when you can write a paper on "How a Weak Economy Affects the Quality of College Life"? It's always more fun to write about what you're close to.

Writing About What You Know

When Joyce was assigned a paper in her sociology class, she had to write ten pages on any issue in sociology that she wanted. In order to work hard on the project, Joyce decided that she should write about a topic that especially interested her. She decided to write about the assimilation of German immigrants in New York City in the early 1900s because her grandparents had immigrated from Germany during that period. Joyce already knew something about the subject, and she remembered bits of information and anecdotes from stories told at family reunions and holiday get-togethers. Joyce spent several days working on her sociology paper because she was also learning about her own background.

You might worry that you're taking the easy way out by selecting a topic that already appeals to you. Why not learn from new research? This is a good question. You should, by all means, choose a topic that will teach you about something of which you have no knowledge, but only try this when you can afford the time. If you're in a rush, play it safe.

Broad vs. Specific Topics

Preparing a four-page essay on American history is probably easier than writing a four-page essay on world history. When you select topics for a paper, keep in mind how broad or specific the subject is. Although it would be extremely difficult to cover the history of America in four typed pages, it would be *impossible* to discuss the world's history in a paper of the same length. This example illustrates the importance of writing about a subject with special attention to its breadth.

Some students say it's easier to write a paper on a broad subject because you don't have to dig that far to find enough information. Others might say that broad subjects make it difficult to analyze one or two main points in a paper. It is probably true that broad topics are easier to write about in medium- to large-sized research papers, but you will probably end up writing only enough to give a cursory glance at your subject.

When you decide on a topic, consider how much information you'll be able to find and how long the paper has to be. If your topic is too narrow and obscure, you may never have enough information to fill a ten-page paper.

Organizing in the Traditional Way

If you are working on a long research paper or other writing project and you are not starting at the last minute, it makes sense to organize your work in the traditional manner of first collecting sources from the library, creating an outline, taking notes on index cards, writing a rough draft, and then organizing it into a final paper. If your professor doesn't have a special system, buy or borrow one of the highly detailed guides for writing term papers and theses.

These term-paper guides not only tell you the traditional steps toward researching an academic paper, but they also tell you how to footnote and punctuate, as well as how to organize when typing the final draft. If you're not sure whether your school puts out its own booklet on paper writing, ask an older student or a representative in any department. Many departments distribute their own rules of how a paper or essay should be completed. It only makes sense to follow the rules that they prefer.

Of course it might not be possible to use a traditional method when you only have a day or two to write the paper. You may have to skip the rough draft, or even skip the note taking. At the end of this chapter, you will find out how to write a paper in a day or less.

Library Resources That Will Save You Time

Throughout the library and bookstore, there are dozens of resources that will save you time while working on a paper. You should already have the simplest resources like a dictionary and a thesaurus that let you find the right words when you need them. Another resource that many college students feel they're above using is the encyclopedia. Most students think that the encyclopedia was for high-school papers and reports only. They think that it is now much too basic. One reason why all of these people think this is that the encyclopedia is so practical and easy to use. No matter what subject you are writing about, you can generally find an encyclopedia article that will help you. The benefit of a good encyclopedia like *Encyclopaedia Brittanica* or *World Book Encyclopedia* is that you can quickly get an overview of your topic plus a bibliography to locate other related sources.

Some of the more specialized resources that will ease your paper-writing pressures include the infamous Monarch Notes and Cliff Notes. There is no doubt that these guides will be frowned upon by your professors, but you may need them to speed things up a little. These two resources are available for novels and other major written works. They give plot summaries, character description, and a short analysis of each chapter. Why are these book summaries frowned upon when they are such helpful supplementary reading? Because too many students use these book summaries instead of reading the entire primary text. The critical analysis that is given in a summary is usually written by a college professor, but it is by no means a substitute for reading the original book itself. If you do buy the Monarch Notes or Cliff Notes (no self-respecting library would have them), it's best not to be seen with them.

Depending on your area of study, there are literally dozens of similar resources that will shorten the time required to write a paper. If your school places them on file, you may want to use old theses as background reading for your papers. A thesis that relates to the topic of your paper will supply a bibliography of sources that you may not have known about. Whatever resources you need, a library reference room can help you immensely.

Plagiarism

Whenever you write papers or essays for courses, make sure you understand the rules about documenting your sources. Each year many students are accused of taking information verbatim from books, articles and other papers without explaining that it was created by someone else. This act is called plagiarism, and many colleges will suspend or expel students who are guilty of it. Not only can you be punished by your school, but publishers and authors have the right to sue you if you take their copyrighted material and don't give them credit for it.

Making Papers Look Better than They Are

There are many reasons why you might have to make your paper look a little better than it is. Perhaps it isn't long enough or is too long. There are all sorts of ways to "work with" a paper and get it into a form that impresses a professor.

When Jason finished his religion paper, he realized he was three pages short of the required length. He looked through his notes for more information, but there was nothing more that he could say about his topic. In order to make his paper appear longer, Jason tried several techniques. He first read through the paper and added subheadings for separate sections. Since he had to skip an extra line or two to set off the headings, he used up more space. Jason also realized that his typewriter had a very small typeface (elite, which runs twelve characters to the inch), so that words took up less space than they would if he had used a typewriter with a pica-sized typeface (ten characters to the inch). When he retyped the paper on a pica typewriter, his paper used one and one-half more pages. In order to make the paper just a bit longer, Jason widened his margin by three spaces and added a small chart to the text. With these adjustments and additions, his paper ended up being the perfect length.

There are all sorts of ways to increase the length of your paper. If you find you've fallen under the suggested length, don't panic—try some of the strategies used above. You may even try putting your footnotes within the text, at the bottom of each page, instead of in a separate section at the end. Since the numbered pages never include a separate bibliography and footnotes page, it's better to put the footnotes in the text when your paper needs to be longer. Whatever you do, don't resort to padding your paper with superfluous or unrelated information. Professors are quick to spot information that is just a cut above chitchat. It's sometimes better to be just one or two pages short in length than to ruin a good paper with miscellaneous information.

Another important technique that you should know about when writing papers is being able to visually enhance your paper. Believe it or not, neatness counts. A paper which is full of typing mistakes will distract your teacher and irritate him enough to give you a lower grade. Just as this will hurt your grade, there are ways to enhance your paper and grade simultaneously. First of all, always use a typewriter ribbon that prints sharply and very dark. Nothing is more annoying to a professor with weak eyes than a paper which is too light to read without a bright light and a magnifying glass. The next suggestion is to use high-quality typing paper with 25 percent rag content. This paper not only looks good, but it actually feels good in your hands. Erasable bond also enhances a paper while making it easy for you; the paper has a shiny finish on it and makes your work look even better, although the type can smear. Also, be sure the letters on the typewriter are clear. A paper with solid *e*'s and *o*'s looks terrible.

Using the Vocabulary Professors Love

No matter what subject you're studying, there are certain words or phrases that are unique to that field. Remarks like "spiritual symbolism" or "didactic verse" are bound to be found in English papers, whereas words like "coefficients" and "variable" are likely to show up in an economics paper. If you familiarize yourself with the jargon of a particular subject, your papers will appear more professional.

There are also phrases that should generally be left *out* of certain papers. Remarks like "I think that . . ." or "You could probably guess that . . ." are rarely appropriate. Also, one should remember to avoid using contractions or slang terms in a formal paper. If you are unsure of a word, check the dictionary.

Getting It Typed

No matter where you go to college or what topics you choose to study, you should have some typing skills. If you are ever caught writing a paper at the last minute, you'll be in trouble unless you know how to type. On the other hand, if you finish writing your papers in advance, there will always be a few people on campus who will type them for you. The going rate is about $1.25 or $1.50 per page. It will cost you more if you have a paper with charts and graphs. If you can't find a student who types papers, there are often secretaries who will do them in their spare time.

Buying Papers and Cheating

Believe it or not, there are actually businesses that sell made-to-order research papers. You would think that this would be against the law, but it isn't. Buying papers, cheating, and plagiarizing from other works may seem like the easy way out, but it's absolutely inexcusable. If you cannot finish a paper on time, hand it in late. You should *never* take dishonest steps like these. Not only are you cheating yourself out of a learning experience, but you're also being unfair to your classmates. Most of all, if you get caught, you can be thrown out of college for good. And you ought to know that plenty of students get caught every year.

Writing a Paper in One Night or Less

Yes, it can be done. Don't let anyone tell you that you can't write a fifteen-page paper in one day. There have been stories of people who researched a thesis in one day, wrote it that evening, and handed each page to a typist who sat next to them. Although you may not want to try this on purpose, you may be forced into a situation where you'll have to know how to do it. Here is what you do:

How to Pull an All-Nighter

1. First, have a glass of orange juice and a vitamin pill. You're going to be up late, so you don't want to use up all of your energy and body's strength.

2. Next, you should have a friend run to the store to get enough food to allow you to miss lunch and dinner. Avoid junk food, but don't forget coffee or tea. Eat food with lots of protein—like cheese, nuts, or lunchmeat—and avoid sweet or starchy foods as they tend to make you sleepy.

3. Since you have to forget about sleeping, it may be best to move yourself into a setting that discourages sleep (your kitchen, bathroom floor, etc.).

4. If you have the research on note cards, start writing the *final* draft right now. You can always pick up mistakes when you're typing the paper. (If you have not done the research yet, go to number 6.)

5. Once you have worked for an hour or so, stop and figure out how many hours you have left. Then figure out how many pages you must write and type per hour in order to finish *one hour before* the paper is due. You will need this extra hour for typing bibliography, footnotes, and cover sheet, as well as to copy-read, make a Xerox, and get it to the professor's office. (Continue to number 7.)

6. If you have not researched your paper yet, be realistic. Can you finish this paper on time? If you come up with a "Yes" or "I must," then you *can* finish it. If you have your books in front of you, start drawing up an outline for the paper. Then write a thesis paragraph—it will help you get your thoughts in order. Next, turn to the table of contents of each book and see which two or three books will be most helpful. Start taking notes from as few books as possible. You can always go back to the others for *supporting* information. (Return to number 5; then continue to number 7.)

7. Once you have figured out how much work you must complete in an hour, stick to your schedule. Write fiercely. If you feel yourself falling asleep, drink coffee or tea without sugar. It may taste bad, but the caffeine will keep you going. Whatever you do, *don't* take a nap.

8. When you're done with typing the text, get started on your bibliography. You don't have to write it out first.

9. In the remaining hour, copy-read for mistakes. This is extremely important if you really want to show the

teacher that you did *not* write this paper overnight. (No one ever copy-reads after finishing a paper a half hour before the deadline.)

10. During your last minutes, add the cover sheet and put *yesterday's* date on it. This makes the observant professor think that you had it done so early that you forgot the proper date. Now get a photocopy (take no chances) and hand it in!

8

GETTING GOOD
GRADES BY
USING THE RULES

Even if you have an incredible IQ, enjoy your courses, and do all of the assigned reading, you still aren't assured of getting an A. Most students think that hard work is the only path to getting a high grade in a course. Why do they think this? Because parents, principals, and teachers have been preaching it for years. Don't believe all of those straight-A students who claim that grades don't matter and insist that they work hard because they enjoy the learning experience. Of course hard work will allow you to learn the material, but there's a long stretch of road between learning the material and getting the professor to award you the grade you want. Chapter 9 will show you how to deal with the teacher when it comes to grading; this chapter will show you how to use your school's grading system to your own advantage.

Knowing When to Drop a Course

Walter was a very bright student. After graduating from high school with an A-minus average, he entered Jones College the following September and signed up for four classes—a normal course load. Like most hardworking students, Walter did all of the reading before lectures, studied all weekend, and participated in class discussions. His economics class was to have three exams during the semester, and the course grade was based entirely on the exams. When Walter took the first exam, he was shocked to find that he got a D minus on it. When the professor noticed Walter's frustration, he asked Walter if he wanted to remain in the class. Because Walter had always done well in high school, he was sure that there was some mistake. He rationalized the D minus by telling himself that he had simply misunderstood some of the questions, and that he would certainly get an A on the next exam.

Although Walter was finding the work increasingly difficult, he didn't want to embarrass himself by dropping out of the class. Once again the professor told him that he could drop out of the course and make it up by taking an extra one next semester. Walter refused. He knew that he was an A student and that he would get a good grade somehow. When the second exam came, Walter had studied twice as hard and yet still did not understand all of the material. He received a C minus on the exam and tried to drop the course. When the teacher explained that he had to remain in the course because the course-drop deadline had already passed, Walter burst into tears.

Many students leave high school with the idea that they are top students in any subject, in any setting. Few of them realize that college is more challenging and that many other students are just as intelligent as they. Walter had the opportunity to drop his class after receiving a D minus, but he made one big mistake. He refused to drop out of the class because he didn't want to embarrass himself.

Don't allow other people's opinion of you prevent you from doing what is necessary. Many students end up getting low grades in advanced classes because they don't want others to see them drop back to a less-advanced class. If you see yourself slipping toward a low grade no matter how hard you study, it's foolish to stay there and wait for the ax to fall. Find out if you can change to a lower-level course or drop it altogether. No one needs a D or an F on a college transcript.

One good way to find out if you should drop a course is by asking the professor how the class grade is determined. If the midterm and final exams are both equal to 50 percent of your grade, you will know where you stand. If you want no less than a B plus in the course and yet receive a D on the midterm, it is unreasonable to think you can end with a B-plus average no matter how well you score on the final. It is simple math: even with an A on the final, the most you can finish with is a C plus or B minus. Be realistic; don't allow yourself to be blinded by how well you used to do in high school.

Using Pass / Fail and Audit Grading

Many colleges have two special types of grading options for students who do not want to receive letter grades of A, B, C, D, or F. Instead, students might select the *pass/fail option* or *audit grading*. Pass/fail grading works simply: a P (pass) is entered on your transcript when you receive a D or above; an F (fail) is placed on your transcript when you fail the course. Some students select this option when they are taking an extra course and don't have the time to work for an A or B. As long as you pass the course, you get a P on the transcript—and no one ever has to know if you had a C-minus average. Most colleges will limit the number of pass/fail courses that you can take. There may be some professors who do not allow their courses to be taken with the pass/fail option because they are concerned that students won't work very hard. These professors have good reason to think that their students will only work enough to slip by.

There is one big problem with the pass/fail grading option. This occurs in schools where there is a deadline date after which the grading option cannot be changed. If the date is early in the semester, you take the chance of changing your grading option to pass/fail before you've had any exams in the course. The worst thing that can happen to you is to receive an A average *after* you have registered the course for pass/fail grading. If the deadline is a stiff one, you'll just have to accept the fact that no one will ever know you had an A average in the course. Your grade point average will show no change because every P is equal, whether it stands for an A minus or a D. Only change a course to pass/fail when you are certain that you can't earn a good grade in it.

The second grading option mentioned earlier is the audit option. Some professors will allow you to sit in on lectures or classes whenever you want. If at the end of the year you take the final exam and pass it, they will give you a grade of Audit. In most colleges, the student who fails an audited course will receive no mark on his transcript. So if you fail, there is no record of your taking the course. This can be very attractive since it removes the pressure that you might feel when taking the final exam, but a transcript that is full of Audit marks on it will never impress an employer or graduate-school admissions officer. They will see that you took the easy way out. You will also lose your incentive to learn more if you rely on audit and pass/fail options. Be wise and save these grading alternatives for when you really need them.

How to Get a Grade Changed

There may be a time when you receive a lower grade than you feel you deserve. When your professor puts the "final" grade on your term paper or even on your report card, don't consider it "final" unless you deserve it. If you're willing to beg, cry, or fight, there's a chance that you can get your professor to change your grade.

Before we continue, you should first understand that there are at least three situations that will prevent you from being able to force your professor to raise your grade. They are:

1. *When you honestly don't deserve a higher grade.* If the teacher gives you a B for the semester and your average is an 80, there is no use fighting. You only get what you earned.

2. *When you receive a grade on an objective exam.* If you have gotten a certain number of questions wrong on a true-false or a multiple-choice exam, there's almost no way to fight it. Unless you can prove that the answer choices or questions were worded incorrectly, don't bother arguing.

3. *When you have a vindictive professor.* If your professor is the type who will strike back at you because you question his grading, you should be careful. Don't argue with a teacher who will subtract more points on later exams simply because you challenged him now.

Now that you know when it's appropriate *not* to argue with a teacher, let's get back to the strategies of how and when to raise your grade.

There are different techniques to be used when you are trying to get an exam, a paper, or a final course grade changed. When arguing a grade on an exam, you'll have the best chance if you argue for points on the subjectively graded section. Here is what Richard did.

When Richard received an 89 on his exam, he was determined to get his teacher to give him one more point (so he would be in the A range). After reading through the exam, he realized that the teacher hadn't made any mathematical errors in subtracting points. Richard then read through the incorrectly answered questions to see if there were any poorly worded phrases. He found two badly worded questions and figured out how he could have misunderstood them and written the wrong answer. The last thing he did was to look at the final essay on the test. He found a place where the professor took off a point for an incorrect historical date. Richard realized that the date was incorrect by only one year.

When Richard took the exam in to the professor, he decided that he wanted only one more point. When he walked in with a big smile, he told the professor that he simply wanted the professor's advice on his incorrect answers. As Richard pointed out the questions that were unfairly marked, he politely suggested that he deserved three more points. He thought that if he asked for three points, he might get at least one or two. When the professor saw how Richard explained his incorrect answers and how "well" Richard accepted his grade, he gave the exam one more point. *Voilà!*

If you want to get an exam grade changed, remember to be polite and ask for one or two more points than you really want. Since a professor always wants to seem in greater control than you, he will bargain down a point or two. If you honestly feel you deserve more than you received, you should always ask for more. The worst that can happen is that the professor will refuse to help you.

When you are debating the grade on a paper, remember that there is little objectivity in the grading system. Most papers use subjective interpretation. Your greatest strength when arguing with a professor is to point out that you were attempting to use a difficult and unusual interpretation. If the professor buys this, he may give you an extra point or two for taking on the challenge.

If you have the misfortune to be a borderline case when your final grade is calculated, you have several options. You can go to the professor now and ask him what grade you deserve, or you can remain silent and take your chances on getting the higher grade. It is better to play it safe and ask what you're going to get. Since it's easier to raise your grade *before* the teacher actually sends it to the registrar's office, it's smarter to ask questions first. If the grade is extremely important to you (e.g., the difference between your graduating with honors), then you should use all of your energies.

Begin with adding up all of your graded assignments. Then ask if you can write an extra-credit paper. Next, find out if you can receive a point or two for class participation. If you still can't get the grade you deserve from the professor, consider going over his head. If there is a department chairperson who might help you, talk to him or her. But remember that once you go over a professor's head you better have a solid case. If you can't prove that you're being cheated, you may be the target for great hostility.

What to Do When a Project Is Late

There are only three ways to deal with a professor when you have not finished a project on time. If you stand the chance of losing credit on the project, you can either (1) hand it in late and suffer the consequences, (2) be honest and ask for an extension, or (3) tell a fib and ask for an extension.

As far as choice number one is concerned, you probably aren't willing to suffer the "consequences." Only a fool would hand in a paper a week late without having received an extension or at least having asked what the penalty would be. When you hand a project in past the deadline without warning the professor, you're slapping him in the face *twice!* One slap is from your inconsiderate assumption that his deadlines mean absolutely nothing to you. The second slap comes from your obvious lack of concern for his wasted time. Now that we've settled that, let's look at our other two alternatives.

You may realize, in advance, that you will not be able to finish a project by its due date. If you have a good reason, tell the professor. It is more likely that he will give you an extension if you ask him before the deadline arrives. This is true because he'll feel more generous when you're the first one to ask for it. If several students have already asked for an extension, he won't be so kind to you.

If you have a bad reason for needing an extension, you may end up telling a lie. This is not recommended, because dishonesty can frequently catch up with you. It may be better to politely beg or force your eyes to tear a bit when trying to gain the professor's sympathy.

9
DEALING
WITH
PROFESSORS

There's more to succeeding in college than just doing your homework. Although it shouldn't be this way, you are going to have to learn how to get along with certain teachers for the sole reason of getting the grades you deserve. While you should always respect your professors and treat them as if they mean well and know best, keep in mind that they are human and can have flaws too. Let's look at some of the teacher types that you should learn to handle.

The Perfect Nag

This professor is a man or a woman whose only worry is that everything be absolutely perfect. That's all the Perfect Nag asks for—just perfection. She will dress plainly but neatly. She wears her hair closely cropped, rarely smiles, has never been late for an appointment, and has no patience to read a thirteen-page paper when she assigned a twelve-page paper. Many students might either attempt to reason with this teacher or simply curse her out. You will quickly see that both responses have no effect on her. She simply does as she pleases.

How to Deal with This Teacher Type. Getting on the good side of this type of teacher may be impossible unless you start early. You can please her by being "overly perfect" in the areas that you can control (e.g., be early for class, sit in the front row, always appear physically neat and eager to learn, follow her term-paper guidelines for length and footnoting, etc.). The Perfect Nag is not a deeply emotional person, so don't think she will be affected by kind gestures or tactful remarks about her sense of humor and her taste in clothes. Just do what she wants, the way she wants and when she wants. And if you're not willing to do at least that, get out of her class.

The Absentminded Wonk

The Wonk probably wears the same pair of mismatched socks for an entire week or one of those plastic shirt-pocket protectors with nine or ten ball-point pens clipped into it. The Wonk forgets everything: he forgets to bring the text to class; he'll forget to grade your tests; he'll even forget the point that he's making in the middle of a sentence. The only thing he won't forget is your name—and that's only because he'll never try to remember it. When taking roll call, he will stare in his attendance book and never look up.

How to Deal with This Teacher Type. You may be worried that you will never be able to earn an A from a teacher who doesn't even notice that you are alive. Don't worry about the apparent coldness of these professors. Although they appear unconcerned about you and may even be insulting, they are simply rude people who don't know any better. One Wonk was known to assign numbers to each of his students' seats in a class of nine people. Instead of saying, "Well, John, can you answer that question?" he would say, "Well, Number Three, can you answer this?" Frightening, isn't it? You may not have a teacher as bad as that, but you certainly stand a chance of being in a class with a teacher who doesn't make an effort to distinguish one student from another. One way to deal with this is to stay around after class and ask questions. Go for extra help, even if you don't need it. In other words, make yourself known by separating yourself from the other students. Remember that it's not that the Wonk dislikes you as a person, he simply cannot deal with *groups* of people. So separate yourself and be noticed.

Mr. Don't Call Me Professor

There must be a million fifty- or sixty-year-old professors who spend more time trying to bridge the generation gap with their tight jeans than they do teaching their course material. Mr. Don't Call Me Professor will tell you how he hates being called Professor as soon as you walk into class. He will either ask you to address him as "Mr. ——— or by his first name. He explains that he dislikes titles and formality. What he really hates is being reminded that he's a lot older than the students around him. He uses all of the hip slang terms that went out of style ten years ago and he will usually wear his hair in a deeply dyed color.

Well, what's so bad about this professor? The problem with him is that he spends the entire semester trying to act like your best friend and showing how he identifies with the "younger generation," and then he tries to nail you in an unbelievably difficult exam. Why does he do this? Basically, to remind you that although he's your "buddy," he's still in control.

How to Deal with This Teacher Type. Don't be taken in by a professor who invites you out for a beer or to the movies. Mr. Don't Call Me Professor is not really trying to be friends with you, he is trying to prove to himself that he isn't so old after all. Keep a distance between yourself and a teacher like this. Call him by the name he prefers, but continue to take the course work seriously. Just because the teacher turns the class time into a wild party every week, don't think the final exam will be anything to celebrate.

The Wicked T.A.

Some professors can be very hard on their students. But there are even more graduate-student teaching assistants

(T.A.'s) who are out for blood. Nothing is worse than the grad student who is trying to prove himself to the head of the department at your expense. The Wicked T.A. will be as tough as he can, just to demonstrate that he has tough standards. Rest assured that the Wicked T.A. will do anything to show the chairman that he would make a wonderful associate professor, and this includes failing a great number of students. Many students have found the head professor of a course a lot easier and fairer than the young teachers who were looking for approval.

How to Deal with This Teacher Type. Get out of the course! That's right. Unless you are willing to break your behind just to get a C, switch into another class. Chances are your "C" work is really deserving of a B plus or more, so why be cheated out of what you deserve simply so this moron can look good?

Finding the Easy Professor

Now that you know which professors to avoid, let's see which teachers you should look for. You may prefer to spend your time searching for the most qualified teachers, but let's face it—qualified teachers are always thrown in front of your face by the school newspaper or the ratings in the registrar's course book. The real challenge is to find the moderately easy teacher. Colleges do their best to either eliminate or hide professors who teach you a modest amount and yet promise to give 90 percent of the class a B plus or better. It is therefore up to you to locate the easy professor on your own.

When Mary began her freshman year, she was told that easy courses and easy professors don't always come together. She learned that there were easy-marking professors who taught courses that utilized difficult concepts, just as there were hard-marking professors who taught Mickey Mouse entry-level courses. In order to find the easy professors, Mary asked her dean for a directory of course evaluations. After deciding which courses interested her, she read through the evaluations, especially noting comments like "This teacher will kick your behind" or "Professor Smith will pass anyone who can spell his name." After combing through this group of student evaluations, Mary spoke to some friends about her list of possible professors. And believe it—any teacher who gives good grades to everyone will certainly be known. So don't hesitate to ask older students for their advice.

Mary's next step in locating professors was to sit in on their smaller classes. She avoided their large lectures since she knew that a professor never exposes his true personality in front of large groups. Mary noticed that certain professors encouraged the students to contribute, and no matter how little the students knew, the teacher smiled and praised incessantly. Jackpot! Mary was finally able to narrow down her pick to three professors. All she had to do now was to meet with them for a five- or ten-minute "chat" during their office hours. Once she "interviewed" the three professors, she saw how lightly they took their subjects. One of them even said that he hated giving low grades and therefore rarely gave less than a B.

Risks of Choosing an Easy Professor

Of course there are certain risks that you take when searching for the easy professor. The most obvious risk is that you will not learn anything in class. Considering the fact that college is supposed to be a place where you learn from scholars, you'll be cheating your parents out of several thousand dollars in tuition bills when you study under the uncommitted professor. Another risk you take by studying solely under simple professors is ending up in a graduate school where teachers have no mercy. If you've been pampered in college, you just may get it socked to you later.

Choosing the Celebrity Professor

Many colleges are able to attract popular professors with national or international reputations. Who wouldn't want to study under a Nobel Prize or Academy Award winner? There are both advantages and disadvantages to studying under famous people.

Perhaps the greatest disadvantage to these notables is their lack of free time when you have questions or need extra help. They may be constantly on the road or so swallowed up by their work that they can't fit you into their busy schedules. Another problem with some of these teachers is that they are not always able to teach. They may know more about their field than anyone else, but they may be unable to convey information or relate to students.

What is probably most important about the celebrity professor is the advantage of being taught by a recognized authority. Not only are most of these people very intelligent and experienced, they may bring a taste of the real world into your classroom. You may even want to share the glamour with your employers by listing your professor on your résumé. It won't hurt.

When and How to Complain About a Professor

What can you do if you end up in a class with a professor that you are having problems with? Leaving the course is not your only alternative. Depending on the problem, you can try to correct it by complaining. What you have to keep in mind, though, is that some complaints are justifiable and some are not.

Justified Complaints

Since professors are human, they make mistakes. But just because they are professors doesn't mean you should let them continue to make these mistakes. These mistakes can be of any form—in teaching, in physical action, and so forth. Here is a sample of complaints that are absolutely justifiable if you want to call down a professor:

- If your professor seems deliberately hostile or antagonistic.
- If your professor does not understand the material and honestly admits it.
- If your professor makes sexual advances on you.
- If your professor blatantly chooses favorite students and treats them differently.
- If your professor constantly misses or cancels class without any warning or explanation.
- If your professor refuses to give you the final grade that your test scores add up to.

Unfair Complaints

If you are worried about being labeled a nag, it can happen if you begin complaining about professors for the wrong reasons. If you start nitpicking about insignificant things, your name will spread through the faculty gossip channels like wildfire. Every professor will either run from you or try to nail you to the wall.

How to Complain

There are many ways to complain about a professor's activities, depending on how serious the complaint is and how much attention and credit you want to receive for pointing the finger. Of course, you can be the martyr and announce to the campus newspaper that the chairman of the physics department is an alcoholic and is not in control of himself during class. Not only could this earn you a lawsuit, it will earn you immediate action from somebody as big as the dean.

Another form of complaint can be made to the dean of the faculty, dean of the college, or head of the professor's department. If you are very brave, you will put the complaint in writing and hope that the professor is not a close friend of the dean. The problem with putting complaints in writing is that you had better be sure of your accusations. When a professor has tenure, he is in a secure enough position to fight your complaint, win, and then strike back by socking it to you on the final paper. Perhaps the best way to make a complaint is orally to a dean who realizes that you only want to give a suggestion to help the teacher. This is the safest method of all, unless you're turned on by leaving scathing anonymous letters in mailboxes. Whatever you decide to do, think before you act. Don't do anything that will hurt *you* or your grade in the end.

Getting the Teacher to Help You

In order to conquer your college years, you're going to need teachers. There's no getting around the fact that they can help you in dozens of ways. Not only can they write your letters of recommendation for graduate schools, but they can also serve as references when you begin job hunting. Many professors have contacts in certain fields that may interest you. Get to know your professors. Talk to them after class and keep in touch during summers and after graduation. Not only can you learn a lot from them, they can remain your friends even after graduation.

Flattering the Teacher (When All Else Fails)

You may never have seen a student give a teacher a shiny red apple or heard a student compliment a professor's "beautiful hairstyle," but rest assured that it happens. What is even more shocking is that the professors usually buy the compliments. Why are they such suckers for flattery? Because they would never think that a student would really sink to using false flattery. College professors are more trusting of students than were your high-school teachers.

When Jill realized that she had between a B plus and an A minus in her English class, she was afraid that the teacher's mood could make her final grade go either way. Instead of resorting to the typical apple-polishing techniques, she used lightweight methods. Whenever the teacher made a joke in class, she was sure to laugh so that he could see. She didn't lose all grace and respect like other students when they turn themselves into the teacher's clown. When the teacher was speaking, Jill took notes with an expression of approval on her face. No matter how boring the class became, she never let her eyes drift from the teacher. Jill made sure that she was not only the first one to class, but also the last to put down her pen when the class was over. Professors like it when they have made you forget that you're late for your next class. Even if you're in a rush, make the teacher think that his or her class is the only thing that matters.

Another way to compliment teachers is by finding out what books or articles they have published. Not only should you read as much as you can, you should also note obscure points that they bring up and casually mention that you happened to run across their book in the library and noticed a remark they made about . . . Some students butter up their professors by being especially nice to their classmates. How many times have your classmates brought in doughnuts for everyone "just because they were on sale at the store down the street"?

The more aggressive students will flatter teachers outside the teacher's office (within hearing distance) or classroom. Don't try this—not only can they see through it, but they will also become angry that you think they are too stupid to realize what you're doing. A more subtle method of complimenting a professor is by writing a glowing recommendation for his or her department file. Even though the files are supposed to be confidential, the good word generally floats back to the professor. And the final lesson in flattering teachers is to make flattering statements in those "anonymous" evaluation forms that you are supposed to give back to them. Not only will they match your handwriting, but they will also be affected by every kind word you say about them.

When a Teacher Is Out to Get You

People may say that you're paranoid, but you may suddenly discover that, for one reason or another, one of your professors is out to fail you. You may notice a certain gleam in his eyes, or you may notice that he makes you the butt of his jokes. Sometimes professors will pick out a student who they think will laugh at their cracks (no matter how offensive) and might appear to dislike the student, even though they don't. If you're sure this is not the case and that the professor has more than hinted that he dislikes you, it's crazy to fight a losing battle. Either raise hell with the dean or switch out of the class.

No matter where you go to school, you will find a few bad professors. But in most cases, you will be pleased with the teachers that you study with. In order to make your college years more pleasant, try to gain from the talents that your professors have to offer. Sooner or later, those talents will become your own as well.

10
CHOOSING
YOUR
MAJOR

As you enter college, you will find that your education will not only be broadened by exploring different subjects, but it will also be focused as you choose a specialty. This specialty is called a *major*. A major is a subject that you have decided to concentrate in once you have become a junior or a senior. By the time you graduate from college, you will have taken more courses in your major than in any other subject, and you will probably be asked to write a major paper or thesis or take a departmental exam that covers all that you have learned in your field.

When you first begin school, you will generally not be required to declare your major unless you have decided to enter a highly specialized field like engineering or architecture. Since areas like these often require an entirely different curriculum, it is usually necessary to begin taking courses in them as soon as you begin your freshman year. As far as other departmental subjects are concerned, most colleges ask you to select them as majors by the end of your sophomore or the beginning of your junior year. In most liberal arts colleges, you will find the following basic departments:

History
English
Mathematics
Political Science
Biology
Art History
Romance Languages
Computer Science
Engineering
Economics
Physics
Slavic Languages
International Relations
Chemistry
Psychology

Comparative Literature
Architecture
Drama
Near Eastern Studies
Music
Anthropology
Classics
Fine Arts
East Asian Studies
Religion
Sociology
Germanic Languages
Philosophy
Statistics
Geology

Although most students choose one of the above departments to major in, others select more specialized fields. If you
attend a large or very wealthy school, you will probably have
more departments or programs to select from. Speak to your
registrar or look in your school's catalogues for these other
areas. You may find areas like:

Women's Studies
Creative Writing
Urban Studies
Geography
Afro-American Studies

Biochemistry
Astrophysics
Communications
Archaeology
American Studies

You may be wondering why a major is necessary. Well, for
one, you won't be able to graduate unless you have one.
Second, concentration in a specific department is your opportunity to spend a lot of time with a subject you enjoy. By the
time you graduate, you will be somewhat of a professional in
this area. Finally, a major can help you steer yourself into the
job market.

Finding Which Majors Are Good for the Job Market

Although you should not select your major on the basis of what is most marketable, you should be aware of how your special area plays a role in landing summer jobs and your ultimate full-time job. But before going any further, it is important to note that if you are planning to attend any type of professional school, such as law school, business school, or medical school, you can major in any field you want. More will be discussed about this later in this chapter. The information provided here primarily concerns those students who will be looking for employment as soon as they graduate.

Almost anyone will tell you that there are certain fields of education that make a student more attractive to employers. While employers are looking for hardworking students who are enthusiastic and intelligent, they primarily want those who have studied subjects that relate to their fields. Few corporations or businesses will be in need of music or philosophy majors, just as a bank will hardly be interested in architecture or physics majors. What it basically comes down to is that your major will rarely hurt you in the job hunt, but it will only help you if it fits in with the employers' needs. Whatever you do, don't listen to friends who tell you not to major in art history because you won't find a job. While there aren't as many jobs that require this type of knowledge, you will find something.

To begin with, you should realize that today's job market has more openings for people in the engineering, computer-science, and banking areas. It therefore follows that students who major in engineering, computer science, economics, and mathematics will have more jobs to choose between. On the other hand, a history major who took several computer-science courses may have a good shot at the same job that a computer-science major wants. Here is an example.

Lucy was an international-relations major in college. She was looking for a job in a large bank, but her roommate warned her that banks wanted only math, statistics, and economics majors. Fortunately, Lucy had taken several upper-level accounting and economics courses, in addition to her studies in international relations. She decided that she would try to sell those courses to bank employers and get her foot in the door. When the small local banks interviewed her, they said that although she had the right economics courses, she was still "just an international-relations major." After thinking it over, Lucy refused to give up—she wanted to work in a bank. She thought of a way that her international-relations background could help her. After speaking to a counselor in her school's job placement office, she collected a list of large international banks. She wrote to them and explained that she concentrated in international relations and had a solid background in economics and accounting. Not only did she receive several offers, but Lucy's salary far exceeded the salaries that the small local banks were paying.

As you can see, your major can help you get in the door of different types of jobs. Every major has an area of employment that can closely correspond to it. To give you an idea of some of the employment possibilities for different subjects, look at the College Major and Employment Chart. Keep in mind that the possibilities are endless—a music major can get a job in a department store training program and that a biology major can get a job on a newspaper.

College and Major Employment Chart

This chart is a sample of some of the possible connections between certain college majors and opportunities in various areas of employment.

You College Major	Employment Opportunities
Economics/Math	Banking, consulting, investment firms, department stores, teaching, accounting
English/Creative Writing	Journalism, book and magazine editing, advertising, public relations

Drama/Art	Acting, television, film production, museum work, interior and exterior decorating, teaching, consulting
Foreign Languages	International organizations, hotels/ banks, and other groups that serve foreigners
Sciences	Research, pharmaceutical companies, medical fields, oil companies
Music	Record production, radio stations, teaching in conservatories, orchestras
Psychology	Career and marriage counseling, staff psychologist in schools and businesses
Religion	Teaching in religious schools, religious TV/radio programming, national religious organizations, religious book publishing

You should now realize that any major can bring you closer to some job in the marketplace. If there is a field that you like, go ahead and study it. If you are creative and persistent, you will always find a job that will fit in with your skills and interests.

Finding What's Interesting to You

As mentioned earlier, you will probably not be responsible for selecting a major until you have finished your sophomore year or begun your junior year. In order to find the right major, it's a good idea to read through your course catalogue and its descriptions of each department. Once you have done this, you may want to stop by the various departmental offices for more detailed information on their courses and their special features. The next thing to do is to sign up for a variety of courses during your freshman and sophomore years so that you can see which subjects interest you most.

Once you have found a subject that you like a lot, register

for a more advanced course in the same subject. If you find that you not only enjoy it but also do well in the area, you're ready for the next step in trying to select your major.

Meet Professors in the Department

Another way to find out more about a department that interests you is to meet some of the professors who teach in it. You may wonder what difference the professors will make, but you should remember that you will end up working under some of them since you'll be taking several (maybe eight or more) courses in the field. By meeting the professors, you'll find out how intelligent, approachable, pompous, friendly, or practical they are.

One way to meet these professors is by visiting the departmental offices and asking if there are any departmental receptions or gatherings that students can attend. Most schools require that each of their departments organize an open gathering of students who are interested in majoring in that field. Although these gatherings or informational meetings are organized primarily for sophomores, a freshman student is usually welcome. When you get to the meeting, ask lots of questions and be sure to meet the professors and upperclassmen in the department.

If your school does not provide informational meetings for students in various departments, find out if there is a departmental adviser who can answer your questions about requirements. You can also call one or two professors and ask them if you could chat during their office hours.

Meeting Upperclassmen in the Department

Another method of learning about a particular academic department is by talking with junior-year or senior-year students who have selected that area of study. They can give you a point of view that professors may not know or may not want to expose to you. You should ask these students what their greatest complaints and compliments are about their respective departments. These students can tell you which courses are the most interesting, which requirements you should fulfill first, how important the department thesis is, and who the best professors are.

Finding What Is Easy

Is there an easy major? You've heard of geology courses that are called Rocks for Jocks, physics courses referred to as Physics for Poets and other guts, superguts, and astroguts. These are the common labels for easy courses. There is still a question whether there really is a department that is easier than all the rest. In most colleges, the answer is yes. The only problem is that the easiest department in one school may be very difficult in another. Since every department has different requirements, you should never assume that because history is easy at Washington University, it will also be easy at Ohio State. Something else you should remember in your own college is that some students find certain courses much easier than other students find the same courses with the same professors. Some fields require that you have a very analytical mind. If you don't think analytically, you'll have problems in those areas—no matter how easy your classmates find the topics.

When selecting a major, you should be warned that an easy major won't guarantee good grades or intellectual enhancement. College is for learning and enjoying what you study. O.K., maybe astrophysics is easier than political science in your school. What if astrophysics is boring? What if the teachers are cold and pompous? What if the other students in the department are obnoxious, or act as if their minds are on another planet? You may end up being bored stiff in a subject for two whole years just because you wanted something that was simple. Here is how Tim found the level of difficulty of a particular department that he thought he'd enjoy.

Tim was interested in both psychology and comparative literature. After reading through the course catalogue, he found that the psychology department required seven upper-level courses, while the comparative-literature department required nine upper-level courses. Tim also learned that if he majored in comparative literature, he would have to be relatively fluent in at least two other languages. Although Tim knew two other languages, he thought it would be difficult to increase his fluency as well as study the literature assignments. He then decided that psychology would be easier for him.

Agnes had a similar dilemma. She didn't know whether to study English or political science. Although she liked them equally, she was influenced by friends who told her to choose English because it would be more basic. Agnes spoke to some students and asked about requirements in both of the departments. She was told that the English department required a seventy-five-page thesis for the senior year and the political science department required her to volunteer a total of six eight-hour working days in a political campaign office.

Agnes also learned that most of the English courses required long term papers, whereas the political science courses generally graded students on the basis of class participation and an occasional quiz. Since she hated writing papers and loved participating in class discussion, Agnes realized English would not be the better major for her.

When deciding between two departments, remember that there are different aspects to examine. "Easy" for one person may mean "difficult" for another. Ask questions and read about requirements before settling on a major that you *think* will be easy for you.

Best Course Majors for Graduate Schools

If you are planning on earning a master's degree in philosophy or a Ph.D. in economics or in Slavic languages, it only makes sense (and it may be required) that you major in that same subject in undergraduate school. The graduate areas that don't require you to have an undergraduate major in the same field are fewer in number. They are counseling, education, social work, and a few others.

As far as professional schools for law, business, and the medical fields are concerned, it really doesn't matter which major you select for your undergraduate schooling. Too often students think that if they want to attend medical school, they should major in biology; or if they plan on going to law school, they should concentrate in political science; and, similarly, if they prefer business school, they should choose economics or accounting as a major. This assumption is very common and absolutely incorrect. No longer do these professional schools look for only certain majors. Plenty of history majors attend business school; law schools accept chemistry majors; medical schools will take art students. Of these three professional schools, only one of them makes a requirement of its applicants as far as undergraduate course work is concerned. Almost every type of school in the health fields (medical, dental, veterinary, public health) requires that you take certain biology, chemistry, physics, and mathematics courses. Outside of these courses, you can take whatever else you want.

If you are planning to attend a graduate or professional school, don't change your major. First read about the requirements of the schools you are interested in and find out if you can simply take the separate courses that they recommend for their applicants.

Requirements for Honors, Awards

Just about every college awards its students for high-quality work that they have done in their major course of study. In order to find out how you can graduate with honors (*cum laude, magna cum laude,* and *summa cum laude*), speak to a departmental adviser and ask about the requirements. In most colleges, there is a required grade point average, and you may also have to complete an application or submit a special letter of recommendation. Don't wait until graduation day to find out that if you had written an extra paper you would have received a special honor or award.

Developing Your Own Major

If you have an interesting idea for a new course of study and your dean gives you permission, you may be able to design your own major. These independent majors are especially helpful if you are preparing for a nontraditional career and want to learn about a special field. Read through your catalogues and ask a professor who has interests similar to yours. Maybe you are interested in scientific journalism. If your school does not have a journalism department, ask the biology department if it would be willing to help you. It may take a lot of time to plan out, and it may require you to combine some of the requirements from two different departments, but special majors can be very rewarding.

11
PARTICIPATING
IN SCHOOL
ACTIVITIES

As you probably discovered in high school, there are dozens of ways to occupy your time in school. Every college has extra-curricular activities. Whether you're interested in sports, politics, or cultural activities, your school is bound to have something for you. Of course your schoolwork comes first at college, but you should have something else by which to release your energies. The most important reason to join an extracurricular group is that you *enjoy* its activities.

Here is a list of college groups and activities that you might consider participating in if your school offers them.

Campus Politics—class government, student-body government, faculty-student liaison, school-store student trustee, academic committee, social-life committee, alumni-class relations, class newsletter, campus Democrats/Republicans

Artistic-Drama—literary magazine, newspaper, yearbook, radio station, music

Social Issues—groups dealing with the arms race, abortion issues, world hunger, race relations, Model United Nations

Civic—Big Brother/Big Sister, volunteering for hospitals, nursing homes, ethnic, religious, cultural groups, tutoring, reading to the blind

These are only a few examples of the many activities you can join. If one of these organizations isn't available at your school, speak to your dean of student affairs and find out if you can organize a group and receive funding. When Nick and his roommate returned to school one fall, they got the idea to fly kites in their spare time. Although it wasn't a very popular sport at their school, a few other students joined them in the activity. Nick realized that it would be a great idea to let other students know about their kite-flying sessions, so he visited the dean's office and asked to register the group as a student organization. The dean explained that once Nick had gotten a petition with ten signatures, he could register and receive a small stipend to get organized.

When Nick got his ten signatures and stipend, he put an advertisement in the school newspaper to increase the membership. It became such a fascination that Nick organized colorful kite competitions each weekend. Not only was it fun, but everyone increased his circle of friends. After two months passed, kite flying was so popular that Nick realized he could capitalize on the new interest. He decided to take some of his money and buy twenty kites wholesale. He sold them at a profit during the weekly kite-flying competition. He had not only started a new activity and a fad, but also a new business.

You may not be able to benefit monetarily from your activities, but you can always use them as a release of mental tension and as a way to meet other people with similar interests. Many students build up a camaraderie among teammates that lasts longer than the friendships that they create through their classes.

Activities for Exercise

If you're concerned about staying healthy or keeping the weight off, you may be looking for activities that require a lot of physical energy. There are many choices for the average student. You can choose one of the team sports that your school offers. The only disadvantages with these sports is that you are generally required to already have a proficiency in the area and to spend a great deal of time with them. Most colleges will have a varsity and junior-varsity level on many sports, but to make either group you must not only be good, but you must also be willing to spend two or three hours each day for practice. That's a lot of time, so you had better be willing to get your schoolwork done in the least amount of time possible.

There is an alternative for those of you who do not have enough time or talent to make junior-varsity or varsity levels. You can participate in intramural sports. This less formal version of sports activity is also good for those who just want to dabble in different areas without having to worry about serious competition. Other activities that provide a lot of exercise include aerobic dancing, ballet, bicycle riding, swimming, running, and playing Frisbee.

Activities for Helping Others

Some people might debate whether class politics should be included in this group of activities. For now, let us include it. Just about every college elects student leaders to represent their concerns in faculty meetings or for running and organizing student-related functions. Unfortunately, campus politics is often seen in a bad light because it sometimes attracts power seekers instead of students who are interested in helping others. Another problem with campus politics is that it is very similar to regular elective politics—the popular students, not the qualified students, are the winners in most elections.

Other activities that can definitely be classified here include student volunteer groups that help in community centers, hospitals, and nursing homes. Many colleges have Big Brother/Big Sister groups that spend time with young children in the community. Your school may even have a peer-to-peer counseling group where students are trained to help other students in their time of need.

Activities for Learning

You may ask how learning can be turned into an exciting activity, but you'd be surprised how many groups are formed around scholarly activities. There may be a debating team at your school that gives you an opportunity to take sides and argue about current issues. Other groups, such as Model United Nations, may have simulated governments and hold conferences to discuss real world problems. Still other groups are formed around well-known scholars. You and your friends may want to start an Edgar Allan Poe reading club in order to read Poe's works and discuss them. Poe may not sound so exciting to you, but there are other authors to choose from.

Another type of learning activity can be one that relates to your ethnic or religious group. Perhaps you would like to bring together other students of your ethnic background and discuss your experiences. You may want to invite lecturers to speak about the subject.

Activities for Informing Others

There probably isn't a college on this planet that lacks some sort of campus newspaper. The good thing about working on a newspaper is that the organization includes not only the reporters who write the articles but also photographers, advertising salespeople, editors, and typists. Newspaper work can be especially exciting if you work on a daily. The only drawback is that it requires an incredible amount of your time. You may also be interested in using your journalistic skills in the campus radio station or on the yearbook staff.

Activities for Entertaining Others

If you play an instrument, you may want to join an orchestra, band, or jazz ensemble. Almost every college has some type of music group that needs student musicians. If you have a football team, you surely have a marching band. When you aren't pleased with the available groups, get some friends to help you start your own. There are just as many opportunities for those students who like to sing. Choir groups perform at concerts with other musicians or unaccompanied, as well as in church.

Perhaps the most popular entertainment activity is theater. Many students have participated in high-school plays or summer stock. Whether it's drama, musicals, comedy, or mime, audition for a part. Not only is it a lot of fun, but you may also discover part of your personality that you never noticed.

Activities to Build Your Résumé

Since employers are interested in your skills, they may be impressed by certain activities in which you have participated. If you are looking for a full-time job on a magazine, the employer is bound to be impressed by the fact that you were the feature editor on your school paper. Similarly, a political campaign office will be pleased to see that you were the president of your class and have experience in running for elections. No matter which activities interest you, they can work to your advantage when you organize your résumé.

Getting to the Top of Organizations

Everybody wants to be the president or chairperson of the group he or she belongs to. But how do you get there? Is it always seniority? In many cases, you need more than seniority in order to become the head of a group or activity. If you want to be captain of the tennis team, you have to be one of the best players on the team, and you have to be liked and respected by the other members. They will like you if you are easy to get along with, and they will respect you if you are responsible and honest.

There are other qualities that can gain you a leadership position. In addition to working hard, you will have to befriend those who select the leader. You will also have to give more of your time, enthusiasm, and patience. When others notice your dedication and abilities, they will perceive you as a leader. Whatever activity you want to lead, you should be ready to accept responsibility for any emergencies that arise.

12
FRIENDSHIPS
AND
DATING

As we discussed very early in this book, you may not get along with every person you meet. Even if you make an effort to speak to everyone on campus, maybe only half will return that friendliness. Many students leave a high school where they knew everyone and everyone knew them. It's hard to adjust to a school where 99 percent of the people don't know you.

If you get along with your roommate, consider yourself lucky, since he or she may be a starting point by which you meet even more friends. A roommate who has a similar personality to your own may have the types of friends that you would like to meet. If the two (or three or four) of you always introduce your friends to each other, you can meet people much more quickly. With some of these acquaintances you may develop superficial relationships, and with others you may become close friends. Once you are over the hurdle of making a small group of friends, your next concern may be to meet a special person to begin a dating relationship.

How to Meet Someone Special

A few students, just like some of your friends back at home, have enough looks, charm, and sophistication to begin all the intimate relationships they could possibly want. Then there are the rest of us who have to suffer cold sweats and self-doubt trying to find a date for next Friday's dance. Every high school had its share of the beautiful crowd. It usually consisted of the homecoming queen, who had her pick of the guys, and the captain of the football team, who went out with a different girl every week. Of course you remember. Well, this is going to continue throughout college, too. It won't be so obvious, since there are more people, more ex–homecoming queens and more ex–football captains competing. Although the beautiful people will remain somewhat in the limelight, there's no reason why you have to be the wallflower at college parties.

In college, there is someone for everyone. Whether you're an athlete, a country bumpkin, a bore, or a flirt, you will surely find someone just like you in the opposite sex. Now, if you're in the single-sex school that has no brother or sister school nearby, you may be wondering how to solve the dating problem. We'll deal with this later in the chapter. If you choose a school with a reasonable male-female ratio, you should have no one to blame but yourself when you're sitting in front of the television or knitting a sweater on a Saturday night.

Joe was a freshman at college who was a fairly outgoing person. He was no longer seeing the girl that he had dated during senior year in high school, so he was free to begin a new relationship with someone. He asked his roommate, Tom, if he knew any girls that he might like to meet. Tom suggested that Joe attend a couple of parties and try to pick someone up. Although he had never done this, Joe thought it was a good idea and waited for the next freshman class bash to meet someone. When Joe entered the loud gymnasium the next Friday night, he was shaken by the rock music and flashing strobe lights. After spending an hour trying to see his way around the dark room, he realized he'd never meet anyone this way. Big, loud parties are a hopeless cause if you are attending them simply to meet people. The rooms are usually too dark and loud to find someone or introduce yourself, and you may end up choosing a person with a seemingly great profile in a dark room only to discover later that you've landed a real gorilla. Not so nice. Of course looks aren't everything, but you said that all through high school—you can do better now.

The next night, Joe was too depressed to go out again. Instead, he decided to wash his clothes in the laundry room in the next dormitory. Since everyone was out on a Saturday night, he thought he would have no problem finding an empty machine. When he got to the laundry room, he found that a girl who lived down the hall from him had the same idea. Although they had never met, it was easy to strike up a conversation in a laundry room. They both knew that the other was there because he/she probably didn't have a date for the parties. Having this much in common, they felt comfortable and began talking. While washing, there was nothing to do except talk, so each had the other one as a captive audience. When the girl's wash was done, Joe offered to help her carry the clothes basket. When he got to her room, they chatted while she put her clothes away. When she was done, Joe finally got up enough nerve to ask her if she wanted to go to the party that had started an hour ago.

Although there are plenty of places to meet new people, the laundry room is one of the best locations. Here are some of the benefits:

- There is an excuse for you and the other person to remain in the same room for at least a half hour.
- Everyone makes small talk when they wash clothes—it's up to you to take it from there.
- People always let down their defenses in such an unpressured situation as a laundry room.
- You can assume that the person is relatively bored if he or she has chosen this time to do their wash, so he or she is probably eager to talk to someone.

There are a few other good places to meet friends and start quick relationships:

In your classes—in a class of fifteen or twenty people, you'll be able to learn everyone's name and perhaps study for tests together.

During your meals—it's possible to sit down at a table of people you don't know.

Quiet mixers—these are good because their sole purpose is to promote small talk between strangers.

On buses, trains—if you sit down next to a student when on your way home or back to school, you have a listener for the whole trip.

In dormitory—next-door neighbors become close when they borrow or lend things, share phones, or study together.

Through your activities—whether you're in a sport or a club, you're bound to find someone with the same interests as you.

At the library—your library probably has a lounge where restless students take their study breaks.

And of course there are places where it's almost impossible to discover intimate friendships. No matter how suave you may be, there are certain situations that do not lend themselves to finding friendships, no matter how hard you try or relaxed you are.

At loud parties—since no one can hear another's voice, it's hard to start casual conversations.

En route to classes, library—people are usually too much in a rush to start conversations when they are going to class.

While shopping—people rarely like to talk when they are shopping. It also looks ridiculous to follow someone around the aisles of a store.

Dating Etiquette at Different Schools

Even if your older brother told you all about dating and sex life at his college fraternity, don't think it will be the same in your college. Some schools have very loose etiquette in that no one comes to parties with dates. In other schools, no one would be caught dead without a partner for the evening. If your college has a lot of fraternities and sororities, the customary way of meeting people is for all of one group to come to the party of another, and then pick matches where you can. If you are of the very sophisticated college group, and perhaps have formal societies or eating clubs, you may have to give a date at least five days' notice.

Whatever you do, don't try to force your own etiquette on a school that lives by another. If the women are accustomed to being treated like ladies, be a gentleman. If the men are used to holding doors or paying for their dates, let them. Don't be offended by an action that is meant as a courtesy. When you begin school, open your eyes to the ways dating is carried on. There is certainly a way to do the proper thing and yet maintain your own standards.

Dealing with Sex

Whether you're attending a single-sex or co-ed school, sex is a large part of the college social scene. The simplest questions about sex usually include: Am I supposed to have sex on the first date? Am I supposed to say no if I am approached? Is it wrong for a girl to seduce a guy? Am I supposed to have sex only with that person with whom I hope to continue a long relationship, or should I sleep around?

These and many other questions are qualified with the idea of what you are *supposed* to do. The only answer to these questions is to do what you feel is right for you. The worst mistake is to run your sex life the way you think that everyone else is doing it.

What you should keep in mind is that there are certain responsibilities and precautions that you should undertake if you want to lead an active sex life. If there is a person that you feel close enough to to have sexual intercourse with, prevent an unwanted pregnancy by using condoms, birth control pills and diaphragms. Condoms can be purchased from a pharmacy, but pills and diaphragms must be prescribed by a doctor. Some college infirmaries might be able to help you with this if you would prefer not to go off campus.

Besides these precautions, you should also use common-sense cleanliness rules. Always wash before and after sex, and use some discretion when having sex with people that you don't know very well. Later we will discuss some of the diseases that can be transmitted through sexual contact.

Sex in the Dormitory Room

You may have a roommate who leads an active sex life that can interfere with your living style. If you and your roommate share the same bedroom, lay down some rules on when he or she will have guests over. It is unreasonable to ask you to sleep elsewhere without giving you advance notice. It is even more unfair to carry on one's sexual adventures with roommates in the upper bunk or on the other side of the room. Work out some reasonable rules that allow both of you to enjoy the rooming situation.

Pregnancy

If a student gets pregnant unintentionally, there is no reason to panic. The first thing to do is to speak to a counselor in your college's infirmary. You will have several options which include abortion, raising the child or putting it up for adoption. Before you make a decision, discuss it with your mate, a counselor and your parents. This is a time when you will need an extra ear and additional support.

Sexually Transmitted Diseases

Because of changing sexual codes, more and more students are having sex with greater frequency. Unfortunately, this increased sexual freedom has also brought with it an increase in the number of people who suffer from bacterial and viral infections.

The most well known venereal disease is gonorrhea. Gonorrhea is caught by roughly two million Americans each year, and it is one of the mildest forms of venereal disease. A more serious one is syphilis. About nine thousand cases of syphilis are reported each year. The primary symptom of these two diseases is inflammation of the urethra or vagina. If you suspect that you have come in contact with either of these diseases, visit your infirmary because they *are* curable.

Another disease is a much more serious and, surprisingly, quite common one. It is called Herpes Simplex and can develop in more than one form. This disease cannot be cured and differs from gonorrhea and syphilis in that it is viral, while the other two are bacterial. A symptom of Herpes is a sore that develops on the genitals or on the mouth. The sore may be closed or open (more serious), but can be transmitted to anyone who touches it. If you suspect that you have contracted the disease, visit a doctor and get a blood test and/or tissue culture.

If you are concerned about your sex life being hindered by the worry of contracting one of these diseases, don't hesitate to ask your partner if he or she is in good health. Sex does not have to become a nightmare if you ask first and take precautions. For more information about Herpes, contact the Herpes Resource Center in Palo Alto, California. They organize support groups as well as distribute information on the disease.

The Pre-Wed Syndrome

"Doctor, lawyer, M.B.A.," said the sophomore as she told her friend about the types of men she'd settle for upon graduation. You laugh. There are men and women in college who are quietly but assiduously looking for wives and husbands. Some will try to snag mates for their money or social status. Others are honestly looking for companionship. And still others realize that their best chance of finding someone is on a college campus, where there are single people their own age who are bound to reach some degree of success in later life. After all, you certainly aren't likely to meet the girl of your dreams handing out shoes at the bowling alley, or the man of your wishes collecting tickets on the train going home for vacation. The "pre-weds" simply believe that you should catch someone when he or she is on the way up in life.

So how can you tell when your girlfriend or boyfriend has caught the pre-wed syndrome?

- When they sacrifice everything for you.
- When they start worrying about "your career."
- When they talk about "our future."
- When they buy you more expensive presents than they would ever buy for themselves.
- When they bring you home to Mom and Dad and then insist that you bring them home to meet *your* parents.
- When they offer to wash your clothes.

These are the telltale signs of the pre-wed who is looking for the pre-med or the perfect match in his or her life. Whatever you do, don't allow someone to tie you down with commitments unless you honestly feel responsible enough to begin a relationship.

Balancing Work and Play

College is almost synonymous with freedom in many students' lives. There are no parents making sure that you get home on time, and there are no teachers who will insist that you keep up with your schoolwork. It's up to you to balance partying with studying. When you have a test tomorrow and a friend has tickets to a hockey game tonight, only *you* can say no.

It's best to decide each week how much time you're going to set aside for entertainment and how much for schoolwork. This simple schedule will remind you what has to be done, even when you're in a restless mood.

Single-Sex Schools

There will obviously be some benefits and some drawbacks to attending an all-male or all-female college. The benefit is that you can grow closer to your "brothers" or "sisters" in a way that will create long-lasting friendships. There is less competition for the attention of the best-looking girl or guy in the class, since there is no guy in a school of girls or girl in a school of guys. The main concern of most students is the major drawback in the single-sex college—finding a date to help build their social life.

Most single-sex colleges have a brother or sister school that gets together for parties and other social functions. It may be difficult to find the right guy or girl when he or she is a few miles away, but it can be done.

13

HANDLING
PERSONAL
CONCERNS

In the last chapter, you learned how to deal with special friendships and dating. But college isn't just one big social gathering. There are reasons why you won't be happy sometimes. Don't prepare yourself with expectations of constant fun and excitement; there's a not-so-bright side to everything. Once you arrive at college, you may be glad to be free of your parents, brothers, sisters, or grandparents. You tell yourself that you can finally deal with your own problems the way that you want. But as soon as a crisis hits, you'll be on the phone looking for sympathy from Mom and Dad. There's no reason to be ashamed of doing this; after all, your parents and family are your ultimate support group.

But what about support while you're at college? How do you handle those situations that family members don't understand or can't change? This chapter will tell you how to handle some of the personal problems that you are bound to face in college.

Dealing with a Bad Social Life

When Jan got to college, she totally immersed herself in schoolwork. She had decided that the best way to conquer college was to get the best grades possible. Whenever she was away from her desk, she felt guilty about not studying. Jan gave herself fifteen minutes for lunch and twenty minutes for dinner, and she cut out breakfast altogether so she could spend more time with her studies. On the weekends, she stayed in the library all night.

One day, Jan's roommate succeeded in dragging her out to a movie. Twenty minutes into the show, Jan hurried out, frantically thinking about how much schoolwork she could be accomplishing. At the end of the semester, Jan received her grades and was quite pleased with her success. When she wanted to celebrate her achievements, she tried to decide whom she should get together with. After considering her situation for a few minutes, she realized there was no one that she could call.

What happened to Jan is very common. She had no one to celebrate with, because she had cut everyone out of her life. No one but Jan herself should have been blamed for her nonexistent social life. But when she complained to her parents, she said that the school was not a very friendly place. We all have the tendency to blame our own mistakes on other people. Of course earning good grades was important to Jan and may be important to you, too, but it is not necessary to sacrifice every waking minute to your schoolwork. Thinking about a history paper or worrying about a math problem set at the movie theater won't improve your grade one bit.

Most students who suffer from a bad social life have no excuse but themselves. If you're one of those people who believe in cutting out friendships in order to study, ask yourself what happens when the studying is all done. What happens when you finally need a date for a party? What happens when you graduate and know only one or two people in your class? What good will your history paper and math problem set be then? Remember that success is only good if you have someone to share it with. Don't cut off the world in order to get one more A on an exam—it isn't worth it. If you don't make the effort to help your own social life, no one else will.

There is a second type of student who is dissatisfied with his social life—Ron is an example of this type. Ever since Ron got to college, he has been comparing it to his high-school days. "I've never seen so many ugly girls," "Everybody here is so phony," "People are too formal around this school," were some of Ron's daily complaints. His parents suggested that he try to accept some of the characteristics of the people and look at their good points. Instead, he walked around the campus with a cynical frown. Nothing compared favorably with his high school; he hated his college.

The more Ron convinced himself that he didn't fit in or that the school was a bad place, the more he found himself on the outside of what was going on. People saw his attitude and avoided his depressing remarks. Of course it's good to realize when people are different from you, but you'll only disappoint yourself if you look only at the bad side of life. When Ron's parents told him to try to get along with people, Ron said he didn't want to conform. What Ron misunderstood was that he didn't have to conform in order to make friends with other people. Whenever you make a sweeping decision that you hate the school, you might as well leave it, because you'll only frustrate yourself and those who are around you.

Liz was attending a college that had recently turned coeducational. Since the school had been all-male for so long, there were very few activities and groups that allowed the handful of women to come together. Although she had her pick of all the guys, Liz also wanted to make some girlfriends whom she could talk with every now and then. Most of the girls were rather shy and therefore never made the effort to call one another. Each of them wanted to call, but each girl told herself, "Why should I have to call her? She can call me first." Although Liz had the same attitude in the beginning, she realized that she wasn't getting anywhere.

Without any formal introduction, Liz simply got on the telephone and called up each of the twenty girls and told them that she was giving a cider-and-doughnuts study break next Saturday afternoon. All of them thought it was a neat idea and asked who else was invited. When she said it would be all girl talk, they all agreed to come. People who are in situations similar to Liz's simply have to break the ice by making the first step. People like her will never suffer from dull social lives, because they work with what they have and are never afraid to make new friends.

Handling Stress and Anxiety

There are all sorts of ways that stress and anxiety can be created. You can create them for yourself, or you can be the victim of someone who intentionally makes others feel uncomfortable or nervous. Because college is full of so many new and pressure-filled experiences, anxiety and stress are major concerns of many students.

When Linda began college, she registered for the regular load and kept up with her classwork during the first two weeks. After joining the field-hockey team, she was approached by the university's women's center and was asked to lead a weekly study group. Linda gladly agreed to take the position. Suddenly, Linda found that she wasn't able to complete all of her weekly schoolwork unless she stayed up until one or two o'clock in the morning. The women's center was taking up too much time. When she was asked to be a volunteer in a four-week drive to raise money for a foster home nearby, she had to refuse because she already had committed too much time to outside activities. The fund-raising chairperson visited Linda and pleaded with her to help out. Although Linda insisted that she just didn't have the time, the chairperson convinced her that it was a good charity and that she shouldn't be so selfish.

Linda finally broke down and agreed to help with the four-week drive. When she received her directions to talk to a hundred people and ask them for money, she practically fell off of her feet. She had already gotten behind in her studies and had committed herself to two other campus organizations. She didn't know what to do. She had physically exhausted herself.

Linda is a typical victim of stress. She has overextended herself by taking up every possible minute of her time in schoolwork and activities. She should have followed her intuition and refused to accept a job with the fund raisers. Even if the activity was for a good cause, it was only going to have a negative effect on her. Frequently you will be asked to join well-meaning activities in college. Don't allow yourself to be pressured into doing things when you really don't have time.

If something is too important to refuse, then you have to be realistic and sacrifice one of your other time commitments. Too often students sacrifice their studies for extracurricular activities. Even though these activities are important, it's necessary to remember why you're at college in the first place. Your parents aren't paying several thousand dollars simply for you to work on the yearbook committee or to be president of your fraternity. Keep your priorities in order.

There is another type of student who commonly becomes the victim of stress. Jordan was a very socially active person. Although he overextended himself, he was different from Linda in that his stress was the result of partying too much. Jordan had no problem completing his schoolwork, because he happened to be exceptionally bright. Instead, his time was taken up by going to every party that took place, on the weekend *and* during the school week. So you might ask how this is stressful. How can someone be strained by enjoying himself?

When Jordan finished his schoolwork on a weekday, he went out immediately to get drunk at a party. He usually stayed out until 2:00 or 3:00 A.M., and then fell right into his bed. With a nine o'clock class each morning, he never got more than five hours of sleep. Yes, he had lots of fun, but he rarely had time for himself to think or regain his energy. A few minutes by yourself can be very helpful because it can allow you to collect your thoughts. When you have a constant need to run from party to party every night, you may actually be running from reality. Speak to a professional about your anxiety. You may simply be trying to avoid facing new situations. The next part of this chapter will tell you about some of the other causes of physical strain.

Causes of Stress

Here is a short list of situations that can frequently cause students to overburden themselves with stress. See if you have experienced any of these situations.

- Taking too many demanding courses
- Sleeping less than seven or eight hours each night
- Overextending yourself in extracurricular activities
- Spending a great deal of time partying and socializing
- Breaking up with a friend or having a fight with someone
- Receiving a very low grade on a test

These are all situations that many students experience in college. If you have recently faced one of them, you may have to slow down a little. It's very easy to burn yourself out when you've got these problems plus the other day-to-day concerns of doing your laundry, cooking your own dinner, and getting along with a roommate.

Symptoms of Stress

Along with the above situations will come at least one or two early symptoms of physical or mental strain. If you recognize any of the following symptoms, slow down and find a counselor or friend who can help you get rid of that source of tension.

- Frequent headaches
- Inability to eat
- Inability to stop eating—some people eat when they're nervous
- Inability to sleep
- Sleeping more than eight hours a day—you may be using sleep as an escape from facing your problems
- Difficulty in concentrating
- Constant and sudden changes in emotion

- Feeling alienated and lonely when you're around others
- Using alcohol or drugs to avoid your problems

Now that you have a list of some common symptoms, let's find out how you can get help.

Counseling and Where to Get it

There are many different types of counselors that you can turn to when you have problems. Never feel that you have to keep all of your problems to yourself. It's always best to let off steam to a friend or professional who understands that you are having a difficult time. Whether your problems come from academic, social, or psychological pressures, there is *always* someone to turn to.

When Marsha began her freshman year, she found that the course work was much too difficult for her. No matter how much time she spent at the library, she continued to receive low grades and fall behind in her work. Marsha became extremely depressed with her grades and found herself crying to her mother and father over the telephone. As the phone calls home became more frequent, Marsha's mother and father said that she should speak to a dean or adviser to get help. Since Marsha was too embarrassed to tell any of her friends about her academic problems, she spoke to the freshman academic adviser and learned that any student who requested one could have a special tutor. Marsha's academic problem was quickly remedied by several confidential meetings with the adviser and her conferences with a tutor.

John was also a freshman, but he had another problem. Although he had a wonderful personality, he felt uncomfortable being one of the only black students in his class. Although he had several close white friends, he didn't want to offend them by pointing out that there were no other black students to meet. He spoke to his resident adviser, who was a white student, and carefully explained his concern. The resident adviser understood John's problem and suggested that he become a member of the college's third-world center, a campus organization that brought together students who were Hispanic, Afro-American, Asian, and of other minority groups.

Many students will face unusual problems that only a very close friend can help them with. When Theresa's boyfriend died in a car accident, she was almost destroyed psychologically. If it hadn't been for her closest friend, Janice, she never would have returned to her classes. Although Janice saw Theresa's problem immediately, she didn't want to interfere unless Theresa asked for her help. Fortunately, Theresa asked Janice if she could help her pull herself together, and Janice quickly came to her friend's side. Not only did Janice help her do her laundry during the next three weeks, but she also insisted that Theresa start attending chapel services as she used to do. When Theresa returned to her religious services, she somehow regained her strength and felt better about her boyfriend's death.

If Theresa had not asked for Janice's help, she might never have gotten it. Even though others may care about you, they may be afraid to interfere unless you open up to them and tell them that you need their help. Don't be afraid to be honest with your friends.

Most colleges provide professional counselors for psychological and sexual as well as academic concerns. If you want advice from them, call them—they are there to help you. If there's a teacher, minister, rabbi, or administrator whom you feel close to, you may want to speak to him or her when you need an open ear.

Alcohol and Drugs

On almost every college campus in the country you will find students who use alcohol and drugs. Although alcohol exists in the less harmful forms of beer and wine, there are many students who indulge in hard liquor like gin, vodka, or whiskey. But just because these alcoholic beverages are available doesn't mean that you have to drink them. If you are of legal age, drink if you want, but be realistic about how much you drink. Some colleges have parties where mixed drinks are sold at prices high enough to discourage drunkenness. But at most colleges alcohol is free at parties and plentiful enough that heavy drinkers and partiers will keep drinking until they are too sick to move. There is a lot of truth to the stories about some fraternities that initiate new student-members by having them drink an incredible amount of alcohol. While these activities may seem fun, they can become dangerous.

Eric had grown up in a very conservative home where alcohol was not permitted. When he got to college, he tried beer for the first time and hated the taste. But he continued to drink it because he saw several attractions in it:

1. He could get back at his parents by breaking their rules.
2. He would be accepted by his beer-drinking friends.
3. He could learn to be more relaxed in social situations.

Eric made several foolish assumptions as he drank only to get drunk. He believed he was getting revenge on his parents by drinking excessively, when it was his grades that suffered and his liver that was being ruined. Eric's next mistake was thinking that he had to drink if he wanted to have any friends. If he had looked around, he would have seen that he didn't have to get drunk to be among friends. Of course, it might have been difficult to meet the same people if he didn't go out to a bar, but Eric could have gotten ginger ale or just a little *less* beer at the bar. If you get yourself pushed into a social situation that "requires" that you be tipsy and you don't really want to get drunk, you should just fake it by alternating your drinks with glasses of club soda and lime, which looks like you're having gin and tonic. If everyone else is drunk, they'll never know you aren't.

Eric's last assumption was that his personality would become more relaxed if he drank. He thought that the effect would be permanent. Many people feel this way, but few of them even consider the fact that drunkenness is just an artificial state. You're not changing your personality by drinking—

you are just modifying it during the period of time while you're drunk. When you become sober again, you'll still have the sense of humor that you had before you had your first sip. Don't expect miracles to come out of a bottle—no matter how much you paid for it.

If you want to drink, don't use Eric's excuses. Drink because you like the taste and the effect. Getting back at your parents and trying to become popular are poor reasons. When you make a goal out of vengeance or competition, you'll end up getting drunk and feeling miserable the next morning.

Many students will use drugs like cocaine, amphetamines, or marijuana for the same reasons that they use alcohol—to have a good time and forget their problems. In many colleges, marijuana is more common than regular cigarettes. Be aware that you may not only be heading for jail when you get caught, but you may be heading for harder drugs as well.

If you are a practical person and are concerned about the abuse of alcohol, you should be aware that alcoholism can begin long before high-school age. You don't have to be forty years old with business and marital problems to begin drinking for the wrong reasons. There are many college students who turn to drugs and alcohol because of academic pressures. Some have been affected by the death of a relative and can find no other relief except from a pill or a bottle. If you know someone who is drinking too much and for the wrong reasons, speak to a counselor at school. There are private and community groups that help these people, no matter how young they are.

Here is some final advice for those students who drink but have some control over their actions:

- Never drink on an empty stomach.
- Never drink alcohol while taking medicine or other drugs.
- Avoid drinking in competitions.
- If you even *think* you're drunk, don't try to drive a car.
- Save your drinking for weekends when you don't have classes the next morning.

Religious Worship

It may seem odd that religion should be included in this chapter, but for many of us religious worship is a personal concern that we don't share with everyone. If you are of a certain faith and have friends that follow another faith, don't feel obligated to give up yours in order to fit in with them. Many students reach college and meet people who have very little knowledge of other religions. If this happens to you, try to introduce your religion to them by inviting them to services at your church or temple. If they learn more about your religion, they will have fewer mysteries to worry about.

Another situation that happens to many students is that they neglect their religion because they have less free time. If you believe in a religion, you should never neglect it because you have an extra exam or paper to prepare. If you budget your time properly, religious worship will never have to be an activity that is reserved for vacations. If you feel strongly about it, make time for it.

When You Feel Like Dropping Out

No matter how old you are, you've probably heard stories of students dropping out of college when the pressure gets too great. If you ever hear yourself mention such a thing to a friend, you should slow down and eliminate some of your extra activities. Don't allow yourself to become so overburdened that you just give up on everything—just give up on the less important things first. Once you've thought about your priorities, you'll see that it's much better to give up your position as captain of the swimming team than it is to drop out of college entirely.

There are, however, some positive aspects to dropping out of school for a limited time. This "stopping out" may give you a chance to work in the "real world" and see what it is that you want from college and from life. Many students plod on blindly, not knowing why they are going to school. You may find that a year off from college will allow you to appreciate it more when you return. And that work experience will be beneficial on your résumé when you finally graduate.

Another point that should be mentioned here is the act of *transferring*. If for some reason you are dissatisfied with your college, you may want to try another school. Before you decide to transfer, it's a good idea to talk the idea over with your parents, your deans and even your friends at other schools. Probably the worst, and yet most common, reason for transferring is dissatisfaction with the campus social life. Although social life is important, you should be warned that almost every college transfer application is going to ask you why you are transferring. The answer they are looking for is one that includes *academics*. Admissions officers are looking for students who are primarily concerned with the best academic curriculum.

When you get ready to transfer, try to do it after your sophomore year. Few colleges will accept a student who only has to complete the senior year. Ask for the application around September and get it in by January. Although you won't have to retake any standardized tests, the rest of the process is the same as it was the first time around.

14
FINDING
TERM-TIME
EMPLOYMENT

No matter where you go to college, there are many students who hold jobs on campus. Although these part-time jobs don't pay that much money, they allow you to gain responsibility and give you a chance to get away from your schoolwork every now and then.

There are literally dozens of places where students can find jobs without leaving the campus. Although most students work in their school's dining hall, there are other offices and groups on campus where you can also work. Here is a sample of the possible jobs that you might find:

Library—circulation-desk worker, clerical assistant, shelver, card cataloguer

Departmental offices—clerical work (typing, computerizing files)

Building services—security guard, maintenance

Registrar—clerical work, editing course-evaluation books

University store—salesclerk

Infirmary—candy striper, emergency switchboard

Student center—cash register, kitchen cook, clean up

There are many other offices to contact for positions; for example, the admissions office, the gymnasium, the auditorium, the chapel, the museum, the alumni office.

In addition to these particular offices, your school might offer student-run agencies. Maybe there is a pizza-delivery agency or beer-mug agency that employs students to work in its on-campus offices or to deliver its products and services. The best way to find out what is available on campus is by looking through the university's main directory of offices and divisions. You probably know that your college has a geology library, but you may not know that it has a special office and staff that are employed to organize class reunions.

Once you have learned all of the various groups and departments on campus, visit the job or career placement office. This office often employs counselors who can refer you to various job openings on campus. If there isn't an available counselor, look for a special book or bulletin board where job offers are posted. These postings may provide the name of a particular office to apply to or a person to phone. The next place to look for job opportunities is in your student-employment office.

Many colleges have a student-employment office that is responsible for finding on-campus jobs for financial-aid students. If you happen to be receiving financial aid, find out if the employment office is required to place you in a position. Keep in mind, though, that any job that is found for you may not be as exciting as a job that you might find on your own.

Deciding What You Want to Do

Now that you know the possible places you can work in, think about what you might want to do in those places. Do you want to shelve books? Serve food? Give orders? Deliver items on foot?

Although many students serve food in the dining hall, you may not like the idea of slopping gravy and peas on the plates of obnoxious classmates. You may prefer having a job where you will be answering the phone, filing, or using your typing skills. When Laurie began college, she decided that she *did not* want a job where she would be working with other students. Although she had no professional office skills, she was very artistic. Laurie called up a few administrative offices and asked them if they needed someone to draw up posters to advertise meetings and other functions on campus. Laurie got a response from the alumni office on her campus. Since the office was always organizing alumni reunions, it was in constant need of fliers and mailers. Laurie was able to work on her own time, in her own room, while also using a talent that she was proud of.

Everyone has a talent for something. If you have a great voice, the college radio station may want to hire you to tape advertisements. If you are an excellent computer programmer, find out if there's an office on campus that needs its files computerized. Be innovative and persistent.

One popular craze at many colleges is the student agency. These small businesses specialize in areas that help serve students and other members of the college community. If your school doesn't have one of the following agencies, consider starting it on campus.

student-ring agency	clothing agency
pizza-delivery agency	newspaper agency
hot-dog agency	magazine agency
birthday-cake agency	refrigerator agency
typing agency	furniture agency
student delivery agency	beer-mug agency

Each of these minibusinesses provide a way for you to earn extra money. If your college is willing, you may ask it to provide a central office where the agencies can have telephones and mailboxes.

You may also want to look at an on-campus job as some type of training for your future. If you always dreamed of working in a bank when you graduate, consider working in the university controller's office. Working in an office that deals specifically with money may prepare you for the world of banking. Think about what you want to do after college. Maybe there's a job on campus that can help you prepare.

Another important consideration when selecting a job is the amount of money that it pays. Colleges that provide jobs for financial-aid students may also set a specific hourly wage for students, no matter what job they hold. If your college allows different wages for different jobs, find out which jobs pay the most. Once you figure how much money you need to earn and how many hours you can work each week, you can decide how high an hourly wage you need. Although you probably won't have a big choice between your job and its wages, don't be afraid to ask for more money. If the job pays $4.00 an hour, you can certainly ask for $4.25.

Once you are satisfied with your wages, you can decide on your working schedule. Most students work ten to twelve hours per week. If you have a very tiring job, you may want to work fewer hours. Be realistic about your time and decide if you can sacrifice your study time for your job.

Think About Your Résumé

Once you have decided which types of jobs interest you, you should decide which ones are *best* for you. When we say "best," we mean that you should consider what the job offers in terms of meaningful training or experience, as well as wages. While delivering pizzas might be a lot of fun, it may mean absolutely nothing when you list it on your résumé. It may seem like too much to worry about, but when you interview for jobs in the future, you will be asked to discuss your on-campus job. An employer who hears about how you sliced sausages for pizzas would much rather listen to a student's experiences as an aide at the library's circulation desk. See the section "Tips for Résumés," in Chapter 16, for a sample résumé.

How to Get the Job

When you have compiled a list of possible campus employers, call them individually and introduce yourself. If you were referred by a professor or administrator, don't be afraid to drop names. Employers feel more assured of your talents if you come to them by way of a respected faculty member. When you telephone the employer, never ask if he or she needs a student worker. Asking a question like this makes it easy for an employer to give a quick "No, thank you" and hang up. What you should do is politely insist that you have always wanted to work in a geology library and would love to come over to chat for a few minutes.

Usually the employer will be taken off guard by your enthusiasm and agree to see you for a few minutes. Although your meeting is supposed to be a quick, casual talk, come dressed well. No jeans or sneakers are allowed here. Also make sure that you bring your résumé. When you get to the employer's office, start the conversation with cheerful remarks. Once the person has relaxed in your company, ask him if there's *anything* that he needs help on in his office. Make it sound as though you would almost be willing to volunteer your services. Although you may need money, volunteering for two or three days might impress the employer enough to hire you on a permanent basis. The last thing to do when talking to the employer is to talk about wages. Make sure you compliment the offices, the efficient staff, the attractive brochure they just put out. No matter how crummy a business or department may be, a boss wants to hear a compliment for his achievements.

If the employer is fairly impressed by you but insists that he does not have enough money, either offer to work on separate projects when they arise, or offer to work at a lower rate. Another way of winning an employer is by making friends or casual acquaintances with other people who work in the office.

If you can get them on your side, they may be able to persuade their boss to take a second look at you.

Finding a Job Near the Campus

If jobs are extremely tight at your college or if you are not satisfied with the rates that on-campus jobs pay students, you may want to work in the community that lies around your school. Many students work in pizza shops, stationery stores, banks, and public libraries. These jobs usually require a formal application process (cover letter, résumé, application forms), but they are usually easy to get since you are generally competing against high-school students in the area.

Other types of jobs that you can perform in the community include baby-sitting, light gardening, and housecleaning. Don't think that you aren't qualified to do some of these things. When a resident is trying to find mature students for hire, he will always take the college worker before the high-school worker. Even if he has to pay more, he will generally prefer to take one with more experience and more education.

Publicizing Your Services

Whether you are advertising a product or a service, never underestimate the benefits of bulletin-board advertising. Check local supermarkets for bulletin boards. These are good places to advertise if you are a baby-sitter or housecleaner or gardener. You may also want to call people by telephone to let them know who you are and what you are doing. The most common ways to advertise a service are by buying space in local papers, sending out fliers through the mail, and simply knocking on doors. The more you show yourself, the better chance you have of being noticed by those who need you.

Getting the Job's Fringe Benefits

Every job offers some type of fringe benefit. Whether you work in an office where employees can make free photocopies or in a library where you get to study your homework, these benefits are important. Before you turn down a low-paying job, think about the possible benefits that will make up for the small amount of money.

15

MONEY,
MONEY,
MONEY

Although you learned how to earn money through an on-campus job in Chapter 14, only half of your worries are over. Once you get to college, you will not only want to earn money, but you'll also be responsible for managing it. Even if you're a member of the landed gentry or of a billionaire oil family, you should be as concerned about money management as the rest of us not-so-wealthy students. Of course there are students who write or call home to their parents for money every week. Then there are other students who have part-time jobs in order to pay their own expenses.

Joy was a student from a middle-class family. When attending school, she kept a part-time job as a clerical aide in the campus library. Although she only earned about forty-five dollars each week, she wisely deposited it in her checking account at school. Joy knew that if she held on to the money, even for the weekend, she would somehow spend it. Like many college students, she was responsible for paying her monthly telephone bill and providing the money for weekend entertainment out of her paycheck. At the beginning of each week, Joy would make a list of her upcoming expenses and decide how much she would be able to actually save from each paycheck. This list of expenses would discourage her from spending extra money on things she didn't need.

Bank Accounts

If your parents have left you responsible for some of your expenses, it is smart to open a savings or checking account when you arrive at school. Find a bank that is easily accessible. Don't open an account at a location that requires three buses in order to reach it. Since banks realize that college students promise a large business, there is probably one near your campus. Before you select the bank for you, ask some friends or older classmates about the best one. Ask which one is the most helpful to students and which has the fastest service. Although you can easily ask the banks themselves, your friends will know which banks have special features that might be important to consider.

One of the features that you should try to disregard is the prize or gift that the bank will give you for opening an account. These gifts are used only to lure you to a particular bank. Don't be taken in by them. Frequently, they're only there to hide the fact that the interest rates are low or that the service is slow. The gifts may be attractive, but they won't satisfy you later when you realize that you chose the wrong bank.

Once you've spoken to classmates, find out the business hours of the banks and visit them. Make sure that you consider only banks that have convenient hours. You don't want to have to miss a class every time you need to make a transaction. When you get to the bank, look around and note if the tellers seem efficient and cordial. Believe it or not, some bank employees go out of their way to intimidate college students. This can happen in large banks where little consideration is given to the student with a small savings account. Read any literature that the bank distributes on its banking policies. Make sure your money will be insured. Look at the percentage rate of interest, and compare it to that of other banks. While you, of course, would like to have the highest interest rate possible, there are other things to consider. Is there a minimum balance to keep in the account in order to avoid monthly charges? Is there a service where you can withdraw money at night or on weekends? Is there a check-cashing charge?

When you meet with a bank representative, there are certain things that you should know. You should know the difference between a checking and a savings account. The former is an account where you are allowed to write checks against your balance. A checking account rarely pays any interest. The savings account will pay interest and will allow you to withdraw in cash or a bank check. If you're far away from home, it makes more sense to have a checking account, since you may have to pay certain bills that don't allow payment in cash. Each month you will receive the canceled checks that you wrote against your account, and a statement that notes your transactions and balance.

Handling Financial Aid

If you happen to be receiving financial aid in loans or grants, there are many things to be concerned with. There are always forms to be filled out and brochures to request. If you are still in high school, the first person to talk to about financial aid is your guidance counselor. He or she can direct you to the right forms and directories that explain the various types of scholarships and loans. At the end of this book, there is a list of some books that describe specific scholarships. Most students who receive aid are receiving it through the federal government in programs like the Basic Educational Opportunity Grant or the National Direct Student Loan. Although the application requirements for these programs are being constantly altered, there are still many grants for students who can demonstrate need and loans for those who want them.

The loans are extremely attractive because they are offered at low interest rates. The grants are also attractive, but the application procedures can be very discouraging. Many students fail to apply for aid, even though they are eligible to receive it, merely because the applications are long and complicated. What makes them even worse is that you have to fill them out all four years of college. But when you think about it, wouldn't it be better to spend a few hours working on these forms instead of losing the chance to attend the college of your choice? The forms are deliberately confusing, so don't think that you're the only one who's having problems.

Private Scholarships

In addition to government grants and loans, there are also private scholarships that you should consider. Many civic groups, large corporations, and foundations provide scholarships for students who plan to pursue a certain area or who have achieved a certain grade point average in school. Ask your counselor if there are special scholarships for students in your school. Many organizations will sponsor essay competitions as a way to award talented students. If you happen to be a member of a religious or fraternal organization, find out if you are eligible for any awards.

Throughout your hunt for financial aid you should remember that you can only get what you apply for. Don't expect a check to arrive in your mailbox just because you need to pay your tuition. There is no reason to pass up the chance to apply for grants or loans. Too many students cut themselves out of a college education because they are too proud to apply for financial help. This is foolish because it is their taxes which are used to create these awards in the first place. If you need money, apply for it.

Scholarship Search Services

If you need help looking for financial aid, there are many organizations that have been formed to search for scholarships. You can provide one of these services with information on your interests and your religious, ethnic, and cultural affiliations, and, for a fee, it will then provide you with a list of scholarships that you should apply for. These computerized search services will usually promise a minimum number of referrals, but by no means can they guarantee that you will actually win these scholarships.

Special Tips on Saving Money

- Before you buy new books from the school store, ask your friends if they have the ones you need. Perhaps they'll sell them to you at a bargain price.
- Instead of selling your books back to the school store at the end of the year, advertise them on posters around campus. The store will rarely pay you as much as a student would.
- Avoid carrying a lot of money with you. The more you carry, the more you'll have to spend.
- Whenever you receive a paycheck, put it in the bank as soon as possible.
- At the beginning of each week, make a list of your expected expenses so that you don't buy things that you don't really need.
- Try to buy used items whenever you can (furniture, refrigerators, books, records, etc.).
- Avoid lending money if you're too shy to remind others to repay you.

16

SUMMER AND FULL-TIME JOBS

Most college students are not only concerned about working at an on-campus, part-time job, but they also need to find summer jobs and full-time jobs upon graduation. As you begin looking toward the summer or graduation, you may wonder how on earth you will find any type of job when you have almost no experience. Rest assured that you will need some help in your job hunting. The likely place to ask for help is your college's career placement office. As you will find, this office is not only a place to receive counseling, but it is also a direct resource for job hunters.

The College Placement Office

This chapter will give you an idea of what most placement offices can offer you in the area of counseling, job postings, interviews, and directories for various types of positions. Even if your college doesn't have all of these facilities, you should be able to find some of them at another nearby school or community college. Most of these offices are similar to small libraries. They usually have small offices on the sides where they hold interviews between job recruiters and students.

On the shelves, you will usually find many books that give information on topics such as preparing résumés and practicing for the job interview. There are also usually directories and promotional material from various types of businesses around the country. If you have a very active placement office, it may keep an up-to-date directory of your school's alumni. Many colleges will list alumni according to occupation or geographic area and provide addresses if you ever want to write to them and discuss their careers with them.

Another service of the placement office is group and individual counseling. If you aren't sure what type of job you are looking for, there are sometimes group presentations where the staff counselors will present different occupational fields and discuss them with you. Many offices will also provide job-hunting workshops or résumé-writing clinics to show students how to face the job search. There can also be individual counseling if you have a special problem or concern that needs to be answered.

Perhaps the most helpful resource in the entire placement office is the job-postings bulletin board or job-postings notebook. Since employers want to encourage students to apply for summer and full-time jobs, they send specific job-offer material to the placement office and ask that it be posted on bulletin boards or in notebooks. Employers who are especially interested in recruiting students (primarily for full-time jobs) will visit the placement office and interview students on the campus. We'll talk more about on-campus recruiters a little later.

When to Look for Jobs

Since we're talking about both summer jobs and full-time jobs after graduation, there are different times to do different things. As far as summer jobs are concerned, most students start looking in January or February. Actually, the best time to begin the summer-job hunt is during your holiday break in December. If an employer wants a student to begin work at the end of May, he or she will interview you during the early part of spring, so you want to have applied during the winter. Another reason why you want to get an early start is so that you can now exercise the advantages that you finally have over high-school students. Most college students get out of school before high-school students do in the summer, so why not make sure you get to the employers first as well?

When looking for a full-time job, you can never really start too early. If you know as early as junior year that you will be working directly after graduation, it won't hurt to begin collecting information from friends and the placement office on possible positions. If you are like most students, you may want to begin a serious search for jobs during the fall of your senior year.

How to Look for Jobs

If you start early, as suggested, when looking for summer jobs, the search can be a rather exciting adventure. Before you come home for your December vacation, ask a career counselor if there is a directory that tells where other students have worked in past summers. This list will give you ideas of where to apply if you don't have any ideas of your own. You can also ask classmates yourself where they have worked in the summer. If a particular job interests you, ask for a contact or an address, so that you can get more information.

You might want to check the job-postings bulletin board on campus to see if any employers have sent new information on job offers during the winter, but chances are that it's too early for postings to have been sent. Instead, look for postings that were sent for last year's summer jobs. It is likely that any employer who solicited applications last year will also be soliciting them this year. Contact the employer now and get a jump on other applicants. During your summer-job search, try to look for jobs that will not only be interesting but will also guide you toward the career you are considering.

Locating a full-time job is a bit more complicated than looking for the average summer job. Since your first job can often determine where you will live after graduation, be aware of the possible locations of your prospective employers. If you want to live in the Chicago area, it doesn't make sense to apply for a job in a business that is located in Texas.

When Grace started looking for a full-time job, she first went to a résumé-writing workshop and put all of her accomplishments in a neat résumé format. Since she knew that she wanted to work for a magazine in the New York area, she looked in the Manhattan phone book under Magazine Publishers to compile a list of potential employers. Instead of writing letters to the personnel offices, Grace telephoned them individually and introduced herself. Although few of the employers were encouraging when Grace gave her two-minute introduction, she was able to follow the phone call up with a copy of her résumé and a typed cover letter which started off with: "Dear Mr. Smith, Thank you for speaking to me on the phone last week about *Sassy Magazine*'s editorial department . . ." The phone call gave her a name with which to address the letter. In the letter, she also asked for an interview. For more information on the cover letter, résumé, and interview, see the "Tips for . . ." section in this chapter.

Remember that you should always read as much as you can about a company before you apply to work for it. Find out the degree requirements of the position and the average salary offers as well as one's chances for advancement in the position.

On-Campus Recruiters

As mentioned earlier, many placement offices host recruiters from companies across the country to interview students for job openings. What you should do to find out which businesses are visiting during the year is to ask your placement office for a list of the companies, their respective representatives, and the dates on which they will be arriving. The reason why this is so important is that each interviewer will usually give only ten to fifteen individual interviews. Since these twenty-minute or half-hour interviews are assigned on a first-come, first-served basis, it's important that you sign up as soon as possible.

Since you will have to present your résumé at your interview, don't forget to look at the "Tips for . . ." section of this chapter. Your résumé has to be in winning form and your interview has to run smoothly if you want the recruiter to make you an offer.

How Teachers Can Help

Everyone who is over the age of twenty-five has friends somewhere in the job world. Your teachers are great resources when you begin looking for jobs. If you feel close to a particular professor, let him or her know that you are looking for a job. If the professor knows anyone in that line of business, he may let you drop his name when calling. If you aren't very close to a particular professor, you can casually mention how much time you've spent looking for a job. If the professor doesn't pick up your lead, you may want to be more forceful. It can't hurt.

Tips for Résumés

- Keep your résumé to one page in length.
- Only list your grade point average if it is a B plus or above.
- Emphasize headings by capitalizing and underlining.
- Don't list your height, age, weight, ethnic status, health, religion, or marital status.
- Use active verbs so that you seem like an enthusiastic person.
- Avoid using full sentences in descriptions.
- List address and phone number of home and school.

Tips for Cover Letters

- Always address the letter to a specific person. Never use "Dear Sir" or "To Whom It May Concern."

- Catch the person's attention in the first line or two.
- Make sure you don't sound pompous.
- Keep the letter short (three to four paragraphs).
- Ask for an interview near the end.
- Always put your address and phone number in the letter.
- Never use photocopied letters or form letters.
- Always type the letter. Avoid the handwritten personal approach.

Tips for Interviews

- Always prepare yourself by reading about the company you're going to interview with.
- Think of some questions that you want to ask.
- Remember to smile and be enthusiastic.
- Watch for signs of when the interviewer is becoming bored.
- Show your sincerity by shaking the interviewer's hand and by keeping close eye contact.
- Bring two extra copies of your résumé. One is for the interviewer and the other is to help you guide the conversation.
- Dress nicely, but don't wear anything that distracts or that makes you look frivolous.
- Avoid using slang terms.
- After your interview, send a thank-you note to the recruiter. This not only shows your appreciation for his time, but it also gets your name across his desk one more time.

These tips should help you put your job hunt into an organized fashion. As long as you don't procrastinate and do make use of counselors and the placement-office directories, you should have no problem finding the job that's right for you.

MARTHA SPENCE

421 Brown Hall   58 Pine Avenue
Georgia State University   New Haven, Connecticut
University Plaza   (203) 549-6851
Atlanta, Georgia 30303
(404) 658-2112

Education: Georgia State University, class of 1985

Major: Art History
Thesis Topic: A Study of the Hughes Museum's Medieval
   Sculptures
Other courses included: Basic Economics, Architecture,
   American History, Foreign Policy, Dance.
Other Educational Experience: Summer of '82 spent
   studying Italian and Art in Florence.

Hording High School, New Haven, CT, 1981

Extracurriculars:

Varsity Field Hockey, Campus Fund Drive Solicitor, Intramural Sports.

Discipline Committee, St. Luke's Society, Student Life
   Committee, Social Committee.

Work Experience:

6/84–8/84   Intern, The Solomon R. Hughes Museum, New York,
            Registrar Department.

2/84–6/84   Volunteer, Georgia State unit of Recording for the
            Blind, checked and monitored tapes.

2/82–6/82   Intern, Division of Youth and Family Services,
            Atlanta, GA. I worked on a project concerning the
            mainstreaming of handicapped children into the
            public school system.

6/81–8/81   Short-order cook, Seafood restaurant,
            Edgartown, MA.

6/80–8/80   Teacher's Aide, Horizons Summer Program,
            New Canaan, CT. Taught remedial reading and math,
            supervised arts and crafts and water sports at
            program for underprivileged children.

6/79–8/79   Organized and Directed art sessions, program above.

Special Skills and Interests:

Athletics, outdoor activities, moderately proficient reading
   of French.

References:

Available on request.

Peter Mathews
64 Dudley Hall
Emory University
Atlanta, GA 30322
(404) 329-6123

Mr. Gerald Rogers
Administrative Assistant
Rayburn House Office Building
Washington, D.C. 20008

February 6, 1986

Dear Mr. Rogers:

Thank you for speaking to me over the telephone this past
Thursday morning about summer internships in Representative Greene's office. As I mentioned, I am a political science
major at Emory University and live in Representative Greene's
congressional district. Professor John O'Rourke of the Urban
Affairs Department suggested that I write to you about your
internship program.

As vice president of the junior class and an honor student with
an A-minus average, I believe that I would be a valuable asset
to your office. I am willing to perform any type of clerical
duties, in addition to working on major research projects. Last
summer, I had a demanding internship at the mayor's office in
my hometown, and now I would like to participate in a government office on a larger scale.

Enclosed is my résumé, as well as an article on politics and the
press which I wrote last month for an on-campus journal.
Since I am frequently in the Washington, D.C. area, I hope I can
stop by and introduce myself. Please call me if any of my
material interests you. My school number is listed above. I look
forward to hearing from you.

Sincerely,

Peter Mathews

Barbara Joy Butler
P.O. Box 73
University of Hartford
West Hartford, CT 06117
(203) 762-4385

Ms. Linda Sharp
Greenwood Publishing Inc.
500 Third Avenue
New York, NY 10017

December 17, 1986

Dear Ms. Sharp:

I am a senior at the University of Hartford and am interested in a publishing career. In addition to being senior editor of the Hartford Monthly, a 100-page magazine of news, fiction and features, I am a creative writing major. My career placement office informed me that, in the past, you have hired many Hartford creative writing students as associate editors in your offices. I wanted to express my interest in such a position.

Much of my out-of-class time has been spent in the writing and publishing world. For the last two summers, I worked in the publicity and editorial departments of Woodbury Publishers. As a senior thesis, I am writing a 100-page novella. I was especially attracted to you because I grew up with your company's "Greenwood Junior Book" series, and I always read about your company in the trade journal, Publishers Weekly.

I have attached my résumé and a copy of our magazine, Hartford Monthly (circulation 12,000), for your perusal. I graduate in late May, but I would be happy to stop in for a few minutes at your convenience. I will be in New York City for the next three weeks. My phone number during this period is (212) 235-6734. My number after the three weeks is listed above. I look forward to hearing from you.

Sincerely,

Barbara Joy Butler

17

GRADUATE SCHOOL
AND CAREER
DECISIONS

In the last chapter, you learned how to find the full-time job that comes after graduation. But what if you don't want to work or can't find work after graduation? You may be considering a graduate degree. Perhaps you have a career in mind that absolutely requires that you have a master's degree or a Ph.D. Well, this chapter will provide you with information on the graduate and professional schools that will prepare you for certain careers. You will also find out how your undergraduate years will play a role in your future as you graduate and become an alumnus.

Many students have a vague idea of what occupations interest them once they reach their junior or senior year. Whether they have become attracted to a field by reading literature, speaking to alumni in the career, or working at a summer job in the area, many students are eager to find out what's the next step in preparing for that particular career. If you have absolutely no idea of what interests you as an occupation, it may be wise to speak to a counselor or two at your career-planning office and let them talk to you about your interests. From these conversations, you may get ideas of jobs that may appeal to you.

As mentioned earlier, there are short career inventory tests that examine your personality, interests, and goals in order to suggest occupations that might fit into your personal qualities. While you should never rely solely on a test like this, it can give you some ideas that you may never have considered. One popular exam is the Strong-Campbell Career Inventory. Ask you placement office about it.

Even if you don't know the exact career you are headed for, you may happen to know that you want to continue your education. Let's discuss your options in graduate education.

Graduate Schools

If for some reason you decide to continue your study of history, chemical engineering, or whatever subject, you may consider applying for a master's degree or a Ph.D. You'll be hearing these terms thrown around frequently when graduation time rolls around, so you might as well learn what they mean. A *master's degree* is the second step up from the bachelor's degree. The Ph.D. (or doctorate) is the third step and the highest; it is an abbreviation for Doctor of Philosophy. Although Ph.D. sounds as if it should refer only to a student who is studying philosophy, it applies to almost every single area of study. While the bachelor's degree is always received in an undergraduate college, the master's and Ph.D. can be awarded only by graduate schools. The master's degree usually takes two years to receive, while the Ph.D. may require three or four years, plus time to write a major paper, called a *dissertation*. There are also schools of law, business, and health-related fields that also award graduate degrees, but we will discuss them later in this chapter.

You may end up continuing to study a field because you want to later teach it, or because you like it. Although there are many graduate schools throughout the country that award master's and Ph.D. degrees in the arts and sciences, they are certainly not all the same. Choosing a graduate school can be as complicated as it was to find an undergraduate college.

Selecting the Right School

If you are attending a large university now, you may have a great advantage over a student who attends a small college. For one, your university may happen to award the degree you are seeking. Second, a large university probably has an office that has a large selection of graduate-school catalogues on display. If you already know the area you would like to pursue, you can do what David did.

David was a senior at a large university. He was so fascinated with his studies in sociology that he decided to look into the master's degree program. He visited his sociology department office and asked for information on the course offerings and requirements of the master's degree in sociology. After reading the material, he was almost positive that this was right for him. He spoke to the departmental adviser and asked for a list of graduate students who were in the department, and he called them. Once he had spoken to three of them, he felt a little discouraged. The students told him to look into another graduate school if he really wanted to specialize in sociology. They told him that the graduate professors at other schools were better. Next, David visited the career placement office to find out if there was any book or study that could tell him which universities had a better graduate sociology department.

When reading through a study called the Gorman Report, he was shocked to see that his school's sociology department had an extremely low rating when compared to graduate sociology programs in other schools. He made a list of the better schools and sent away for specific information from each school.

Finding Information on Graduate Schools

As David found, it isn't a good idea to assume that just because your school has given you a good undergraduate education, it will also give you highly rated *graduate* training. Whenever you can, look at books that rate schools and speak to people who attend these schools. Most important, send away for specific catalogues that give details on courses, professors, tuition, and housing. A simple postcard with your return address can be sent to the admissions office of each school. Be sure to let the admissions offices know which department interests you so they can send you the most specific information. When you receive all of the catalogues, compare them and see which ones offer what you're looking for.

What to Look for in a Graduate School

There are many things that make one graduate school different from another. In addition to looking at the various ratings of academic quality, you should look at the faculty and examine their qualifications. Do you recognize any of them as leaders in the field? Are any of them authors of articles or books that you have studied? You may think this is unimportant, but a graduate school is only as good as the faculty that teaches it.

The next thing to look at is the selection of courses. Don't get trapped in a school that offers a small group of courses. Even if you want a degree in psychology and don't think that you want to take a course in animal psychology, you may later realize that it would be a good thing to know about. Since you're going to be in the school for at least two years, studying only *one* subject, you'll want a variety and a choice of what you'll get in that one subject.

If you graduated from college without having to produce a thesis at the end of your last year, don't think it will happen in graduate school. A thesis (or dissertation for Ph.D.'s) is a basic part of your graduate education. When you read through the catalogues, find the section on the thesis and the other academic requirements. Some schools may require that you serve as a teaching assistant for a course, while others may ask you to do independent study or to help a professor on a research project.

Perhaps the most overlooked characteristic of a graduate school is its social environment. Graduate study can become very intense no matter what field you pursue. What can make it even more difficult is selecting a school that has unsociable graduate students on the edge of a university that supplies no alternative social options. When Diane looked into graduate school at Princeton University, she was very excited. She knew that Princeton had one of the best English departments in the country. But what she did not know was that Princeton, like many other schools, places an emphasis on the undergraduate students. Diane got an excellent education as a graduate student at Princeton, but she felt left out in many ways. Had she examined it closer, she would have discovered that the graduate dormitories and dining hall were a good twenty-minute walk from the main campus. She also would have seen that social functions were almost nonexistent for graduate students.

Although Diane thought the trade-off was worth it, you may not. Diane felt that she got the best possible education even though she had to go out of her way to create a social life. If your social life is very important to you, speak to the students who attend the graduate schools of your choice. Don't rely too much on the catalogues in this situation, since the catalogue only tells you the good things. A visit to the campus may help, too, if you want to be sure of the emotional atmosphere and the available facilities on campus.

Entrance Exams

You guessed it! More exams. If you remember the SAT or ACT exams that you took to get into college, there is one designed especially for graduate schools. It is called the Graduate Record Examination (GRE) and can be taken in just about any subject that you want. Most students take this exam sometime during the early part of their senior year.

The GRE tests your knowledge in specific areas. This means one thing—don't walk into the test without preparing. Either buy a GRE review book or visit your placement office to find GRE review material. There is also an application and information packet that you should read before registering for the test. The packet will tell you about the special GRE that tests your general knowledge and aptitude. Although you need not panic about these tests, it is good to know there are guides and review courses that will help you prepare for these exams. If you are disciplined enough to study on your own, you can save a few hundred dollars and avoid the course. (There are other entrance exams for professional school. They will be discussed later in this chapter.)

Applying to Graduate Schools

Once you have sent away for applications, it's a good idea to read through the applications to see what essay questions are similar. This will allow you to use the same essay for certain schools. By the time you've received your GRE scores, you should have your grade point average. Check each graduate school's catalogue and see where you fall as far as your qualifications are concerned. Remember that graduate-school admission is very different from college admission in that your acceptance is determined more by your grades and GRE scores than by anything else. While letters of recommendation and activities are a part of the process, they no longer hold the weight that they did when you applied to colleges. Make sure that you are being realistic about the schools to which you are applying. If you have a B-minus grade point average and all the schools you're applying to are looking for A minus or better, you should try other schools that are looking for your qualifications. At the same time, you should never be discouraged from applying to schools that desire just a little more than what your grades and scores stack up to. You may have held an impressive summer job that makes a difference in your application.

If the schools you are applying to grant interviews, it makes sense to ask for one. Whenever you feel that an interview can aid you in the admissions process, ask to have one with a director or assistant director of admissions. It's important to know, however, that these interviews are taken seriously—they are not social calls. When you are called for an individual interview, you should be prepared to say certain things. Later in this chapter, we'll discuss the best way to handle an admissions interview.

Professional Schools

As students realize that it is getting more difficult to find jobs, they are seeking professional degrees to make themselves more marketable in the job world. If you are interested in law, business, or one of the medicine-related fields, you probably fall into this category. Since each area is handled a little differently, we will discuss each school and its admissions process separately.

Law Schools

Being an attorney may seem glamorous and exciting, but the three-year road to getting a law degree is hardly an easy one. Law schools are very different from the graduate schools discussed earlier in that law schools don't care what your major was in college. There are also no required courses to take in order to gain admission to law schools. The only requirements for law school are a degree from an undergraduate school, a score on the Law School Admissions Test (LSAT), and one or two letters of recommendation with an application. Sounds easy, doesn't it?

The main concern about law school for most applicants is getting into the best or most prestigious schools. Why should this make a difference? Mainly because these students want to work with the highest-paying law firms possible, and in order to be recruited by a good firm, they must attend a good school. Because so many students are primarily concerned about the prestige of a law school, there is fierce competition for the top ten or fifteen law schools.

When selecting a law school, you should follow the same procedure as that used for looking at graduate schools. You should read catalogues and talk to students. The next thing to do is to find out the job-placement information of each school. Every law school keeps a record of where its graduates went. It also keeps a record of how much each graduate is offered for a salary upon graduation. This should make a difference to you since you'll be looking for a job directly after graduation.

You can find a lot of this information from the law-school catalogues, but the best way to learn about it is through your placement office. Most college placement offices invite representatives from law schools to speak to college juniors and seniors. Although interviews are not a part of the admissions process in law schools, many universities will sponsor small group or individual meetings with law-school admission officers. When you speak to these people, ask about their recommended median test scores and grade point averages for applicants.

Law School Admissions Test (LSAT)—Your next step is to register for the LSAT and begin preparing for it. The test is one that is supposed to predict your ability to succeed in the first year of law school. The three- to four-hour exam requires no understanding of law and can be prepared for with an LSAT review book or course. Since many students take the course, you're at an immediate disadvantage if you have no practice when you walk into that test room. It's a good idea to take the exam in late junior year or early senior year. This will allow you a chance to see your score and take the test again if you think you can do better.

Applications—Once you have received your applications, you can start providing the schools with information on the courses you've taken, your activities, summer jobs, and other achievements. Although the essay (or essays) are not as important as grades and scores, you want to spend a great deal of time on it so that you appear to be a well-rounded person.

When Marilyn applied to law schools, she decided to talk about her experiences as a camp counselor, news editor for her school paper, and cocaptain of the softball team. In her essay, she talked about how her activities constantly taught her the importance of leadership and teamwork. Marilyn knew that law schools were very interested in the leadership qualities of applicants, so she told them what they wanted to hear. When you choose your essay topics, don't make them obscure. Talk about something that will tell the admissions people what you're like and what you can bring to their school.

Law School Recommendations—In addition to an essay, you'll probably be responsible for supplying one or two letters of recommendation from professors or other people who know you well. Even if a school doesn't ask for a recommendation, make sure you give it one. A professor who taught you in a course is always your best bet, since he or she can talk about your contributions to the class. You may also want a summer-job employer to write for you.

When you ask people to write letters, it's a good idea to give them your résumé and let them know why you want to attend law school. This will allow them the opportunity to make the recommendation very personal with these small details. Be sure to give each reference a stamped envelope to send the letter in. It's unfair to have them pay when they probably have to write for other students too. If your school offers the service, you may want to have your recommendations placed in a semipermanent file on campus. This will allow you to have the letters sent any time in the future.

Business Schools

Another type of professional school is the graduate business school which awards the ever-popular M.B.A. (Master's in Business Administration). Who are the people who want to earn an M.B.A.? People who are looking to join large corporations, banks, and many consulting groups. The M.B.A. has become extremely popular in the past few years. One benefit to attending business school is that it lasts only two years and yet may allow you to earn several thousand dollars more in the same job than if you only had an undergraduate degree. Business schools, like law schools, are rated by various groups. You should look at these ratings and catalogues as you would for law schools. The main point to keep in mind about business school, though, is that many schools will not accept students directly out of college. Business schools prefer to take students who have had one or two years of work experience.

Applications—Although these schools prefer students who have some full-time work experience, it is customary for students to apply while they are college seniors. Once the admissions staff has looked over your application, they will either accept you immediately, accept you with a deferral statement that says you must first work a year or two, or reject you. So it makes sense to apply first and let the schools make the decision. They will probably base their decision on your summer-job or on-campus work experience. If you happen to be business manager of the school paper, you may have a good chance of being accepted without a year of work experience.

Oddly enough, business schools are generally more interested in your background than are law schools. They generally ask for more essays on your application, and they may frequently ask for additional recommendations (for example, from summer-job employers), whereas law school is primarily concerned with what one or two professors have to say about you.

Graduate Management Admission Test (GMAT)—The GMAT is the test that business schools require you to take before applying. It is supposed to measure one's ability to think systematically. It does not measure your business sense or entrepreneurial talents. The seven- or eight-part exam tests reading comprehension and practical judgment, among other skills. Since the exam generally lasts three hours, most students prepare for it by taking practice exams on their own (with a test guide) or with the aid of a tutoring service. Like the LSAT, the GMAT puts most students under great time pressure; so those students who are accustomed to the format of the exam will probably come out ahead of others who walk into the test without any practice.

Recommendations—As mentioned earlier, business schools prefer to accept those students who have spent one or two years in the work force. Because of this, students should be aware of the fact that recommendations from employers will hold a lot of weight in their applications for admission. If you apply directly from college, you should not only have the normal teacher recommendations sent, but you should also have your summer-job employers write for you. Unfortunately, business schools are not concerned with or that impressed by letters that are sent by employers from non-business-related groups. A summer job with an investment bank will have a greater effect on your application than will a summer job with a music school. The business school's primary concern is that you be familiar with the business world *before* you come to its classrooms.

Medical Schools (and Other Health-Related Schools)

Included in this section are medical, dental, and veterinary schools. If your mother always dreamed of your becoming "my son/daughter the doctor," this section will tell you what you need to know. The health-related professional schools have much different admission requirements from those of law and business schools. To begin with, most medicine-related schools follow a four-year program; and second, they require that you take certain science courses in college. Find out who your school's pre-med adviser is, and ask him or her which science and math courses are required for students interested in medical or other similar schools. You should also know that most health-related fields like medicine and dentistry require internships and residencies with hospitals and clinics after you graduate from school. Any medical student will tell you that becoming a doctor is a sacrifice not only in courses like the infamous college organic chemistry, but also in your graduate education.

When you look into schools to apply to, realize that pre-med students will often apply to fifteen or more schools. Because of the competition, students play it safe and apply to as many schools as they can. What are the admissions decisions based on? Test scores, grades, recommendations, and interviews.

Entrance Exams—There is a different exam for each area of health. The popular ones are the MCAT (Medical College

Admissions Test), the DAT (Dental Aptitude Test), and the
VAT (Veterinary Aptitude Test). You absolutely must prepare
for these tests. It seems ridiculous to say, but the primary
reason to study for these exams is that everyone else is
studying. If you walk into exams like these without any
practice, your mind will be burnt out in the first three hours.
These exams can last as long as six or seven hours!

Applications and Recommendations—When Paul considered
applying to medical school, he heard that it would be to his
advantage to send his application in as early as possible. Since
most pre-med students finish their applications in September
or October of their senior year (at the latest), he sent his during
July and August, before school started.

As many colleges require, Paul's undergraduate school
asked him to have letters of recommendation sent to the pre-
med committee. This committee then combined the letters into
one joint letter and mailed it to the medical schools that Paul
indicated. The secret to applying to medical school is applying
as early as you can complete the forms and line up your
recommenders.

Interviews—Once you have sent your application in, the
admissions committees of most medical schools will review it
and decide if you are qualified to receive an interview. Most
medical schools interview only those students who have impressive grades and scores. This interview is to be taken
seriously. The purpose of it is to weed out the unfeeling pre-
med who merely wants to be a doctor because of the title and
prestige. It sounds cold and unfair, but medical schools are
trying to make sure that their students are sincerely committed
to helping others. Here are some tips:

1. Practice in advance. Think of the questions you might be
asked and consider how you would answer. 2. Dress neatly
and maturely—no sneakers, jeans, gaudy jewelry, or heavy
makeup. 3. Don't bring family or friends with you. 4. Smile
and be enthusiastic. 5. Send a thank-you note after the
interview.

Schools of Social Work

Another type of graduate professional school that continues to be popular in spite of fewer job opportunities is the school of social work. Although many students will begin their practice of social work with a B.S.W. (Bachelor's in Social Work), there are other students who continue their study until they receive an M.S.W. (Master's in Social Work). The reason why this profession continues to attract many students is that it allows a student to combine so many other interests while also helping others. There are social workers who work with the elderly, children, families, the mentally ill, the handicapped, and many other groups. In addition, social workers can work in many different settings: hospitals, schools, business offices, as well as privately in their own homes.

Fellowships

There are still other alternatives to consider when you are about to graduate from college. One popular consideration of students is applying for academic fellowships. These are grants for students either to study in their own country or to travel abroad and study. The grandest fellowship of them all, the Rhodes, is a two-year scholarship to study at Oxford University in England. The process of application is a rigorous one that requires a half-dozen letters of recommendation, an impressive résumé, and a brilliantly written essay. Besides all these, one needs top grades.

There are many other fellowships, such as the Fulbright, Marshall, and Churchill. Ask your dean or placement office about them. They give you an opportunity to pursue a special field while spending none or very little of your own money. Many students receive graduate degrees through these fellowships. Other fellowships also provide work experience in a particular field.

Getting Help from Alumni

If you want advice on what to do after graduation, you may consider speaking to recently graduated alumni. Ask your alumni office if it keeps records of alumni who are in certain graduate schools or particular careers that interest you.

The College Survival Calendar

Being away at college can often cause many worries if you don't have yourself organized. You no longer have Mom and Dad telling you when to study for exams, when to start job hunting, or when to meet with your dean and adviser. Since each year brings new responsibilities, it's important to know when to do what. The College Survival Calendar tells you what things to take care of each month during your college years.

FRESHMAN YEAR

Before School Starts

Contact your roommate(s) and decide who should bring which furnishings for your new room • Start shopping for linen and school supplies before you leave • Prepare for any placement exams administered during orientation • Save your money so you can open a bank account at school

SEPTEMBER–OCTOBER

Try to meet as many students and deans as possible • Talk to older students and read teacher evaluations so you can choose good courses • Discuss any rooming problems with your resident counselor before it gets too late • If you feel you have time, start looking for an on-campus part-time job

NOVEMBER–DECEMBER

Look around and decide which activities or sports you want to join • Drop a note to relatives and friends at home to keep in touch • Start preparing for upcoming final exams • Choose courses for next semester

JANUARY–FEBRUARY

Use holiday vacations to begin your summer-job hunt • Visit your career placement office to find out about summer-job openings • Work hard in this semester's classes by participating in discussions and going for extra help if necessary • For extra cash consider selling last semester's books to a used-book store

MARCH—APRIL

Since spring is also party time, try to balance your work and play • Try to firm up your summer job with interviews and phone calls • Ask one or two of your teachers to write a general recommendation for your file • If your grades are slipping, get a tutor before finals arrive

MAY—JUNE

Prepare for final exams and finish term papers • Find out about your school's storage policy so you don't have to lug all your room furnishings back home • Choose next semester's courses, but meet the professors first • Start your summer job • Make housing arrangements for next year

JULY—AUGUST

Ask your college about summer activities for its alumni and current students • Work hard at your summer job so you can get a good recommendation • Volunteer for a nearby hospital or civic center • Enjoy the summer

SOPHOMORE YEAR

SEPTEMBER—OCTOBER

Since you'll have to declare your major this year, think about which areas appeal to you • Try to gain more responsibility in your extracurricular activity • Stop in on deans and last year's teachers to say hello • Try to make some new friends

NOVEMBER—DECEMBER

Find out about special awards and scholarships that you can apply for • Talk to your academic adviser and think about the best major area of study for you • When choosing next semester's courses, think about graduation requirements • Study extra hard because graduate schools pay attention to the grades from here on

JANUARY—FEBRUARY

Let your friends and teachers know what type of summer job you're looking for • Now is the time to send away for a transfer application if you are not satisfied with your college • Volunteer for a college fund drive or local charity • Consider applying to be a resident counselor

MARCH–APRIL

If academic pressure is getting too much for you, spend less time on your extracurricular activities • Form a study group for your final exams—they're bound to be harder than last year's • Since junior year is the popular time to study abroad, talk to your adviser about overseas opportunities

MAY–JUNE

Calculate your grade point average and scare yourself into working harder • Declare your major • Consider taking a summer course in computer science to make yourself a marketable job applicant • Talk to some older students and ask them about graduate school • Take a summer job that interests you

JULY–AUGUST

Spend some time catching up with old high-school friends • Volunteer a few hours to a nursing home or nonprofit group • Learn how to type if you don't already know how • Hold onto your notes for old courses—you may need them for future exams • Buy school supplies at home—school stores are often overpriced

JUNIOR YEAR

SEPTEMBER–OCTOBER

Visit your career-counseling office and discuss career possibilities • Try to gain a leadership role in your extra-curricular activities • Visit your alumni office and gather names of those who are in an occupation that interests you

NOVEMBER–DECEMBER

Keep your grades up; these grades are the most important if you're planning on more schooling after college • Find out about dates for graduate-school entrance exams • Keep up a good rapport with teachers and deans so you can get recommendations later • Keep in touch with your old summer-job employers

JANUARY–FEBRUARY

Start looking for a summer job in the field that you may ultimately choose as an occupation • Meet with your academic adviser and make sure you are fulfilling all requirements • Put together a new résumé that includes some of your tougher courses and your past jobs • Send away for some graduate-school catalogues • Try to gain a higher standing in your school activities

MARCH—APRIL

Prepare for final exams and decide if you want to write an honors thesis for next year • Ask your favorite teachers if they will write grad-school letters of recommendation • Start researching grants and loans for graduate school

MAY—JUNE

Choose especially challenging courses for next semester so grad schools don't think you're entering senior slump • Sign up for a review course to prepare for GRE, LSAT, GMAT, or other exams • When summer starts, get in touch with college alumni and work on network building • Visit graduate schools that interest you and get interviews • Order a school ring

JULY—AUGUST

Get together with your old high-school friends and find out what they are doing • Have your summer-job employer write a letter of recommendation • If you're writing a senior thesis, consider doing some research on it now

SENIOR YEAR

SEPTEMBER—OCTOBER

Find out how to apply for the awards that are given out at graduation time • Meet with the registrar and make sure your transcript is accurate • Ask the job placement office about job recruiters for full-time positions and summer positions • Start filling out grad-school applications

NOVEMBER—DECEMBER

Study for final exams • Spend time on your job hunt by arranging interviews and sending query letters to employers • Meet with academic adviser when choosing the next semester's classes so you fulfill all the college's requirements • Attend any job fairs or job-hunting seminars that your school or community sponsors • Order cap and gown for graduation

JANUARY—FEBRUARY

If you have saved enough money, look into summer traveling—this is one of the last chances you'll get • Start finding out where classmates are going after graduation—they are the basis for your network • Don't forget to order your class yearbook

MARCH–APRIL

Consider selling your old books and unneeded furnishings in a room sale • Keep up a good rapport with deans and professors by letting them know what you're doing next year • Contact relatives and friends from home to let them know you are graduating • Find out how you can join your college alumni organization • Make sure you've paid all fines and dues to library and school store

MAY–JUNE

Try not to let your grades slip, even though this is the last semester • Get ready for graduation by reserving tickets as well as rooms for visiting family members and friends • Close any bank accounts or charge accounts to university facilities

Selected Reading

COLLEGE LIFE AND COLLEGE ADMISSIONS

Barron's Profiles of American Colleges
   Woodbury, N.Y.: Barron's Educational Series, 1982.
Ten Point Plan for College Acceptance
   Graham, Lawrence. New York: Putnam, 1982.
Peterson's Annual Guide to Undergraduate Study
   Princeton, N.J.: Peterson's Guides, 1982.
Insider's Guide to the Colleges
   Staff of the Yale *Daily News*. New York: Perigee Books, 1981.

FINANCIAL AID AND SCHOLARSHIPS

Financing College Education
   Kohl, Kenneth and Irene. New York: Harper and Row, 1981.
Your Own Financial Aid Factory
   Leider, Robert. Princeton, N.J.: Peterson's Guides, 1980.
The Official College Entrance Examination Board Guide to Financial Aid for Students and Parents
College Entrance Examination Board. New York: Simon and Schuster, 1980.
Cutting College Costs
   Donald, Bruce H. New York: E. P. Dutton, 1982.

STUDY SKILLS AND STUDY GUIDES

Faster Reading Self-Taught
Shefter, Harry. New York: Pocket Books, 1981.
Cliffs Study Guides for Literature
Many authors. Lincoln, Nebraska: Cliffs Preparation Guides, 1982.
Monarch Notes for Literature
Many authors. New York: Monarch Press, 1982.
Barnes and Noble Outlines for Course Subjects
Many authors. New York: Harper and Row, 1982.

WRITING PAPERS AND ESSAYS

A Manual for Writers, 4th ed.
Turabian, Kate L. Chicago: University of Chicago Press, 1973.
The Elements of Style
Strunk, William, and White, E. B. New York: Macmillan, 1979.
Word Power Made Easy
Lewis, Norman. New York: Pocket Books, 1979.

JOBS FOR STUDENTS

The Students Guide to Internships and Fellowships
Students at Amherst College. New York: E. P. Dutton, 1980.
Jobs in the Real World
Graham, Lawrence. New York: Grosset & Dunlap, 1982.
Job Bank Series (different volumes for different parts of U.S.)
Adams, Robert. Brookline, Mass.: Bob Adams, 1982.
International Jobs
Kocher, Eric. Reading, Mass.: Addison-Wesley, 1980.

CAREERS FOR STUDENTS

Discover What You're Best At
Gale, Barry and Linda. New York: Simon and Schuster, 1982.
What Color is Your Parachute?
Bolles, Richard N. Berkeley, Calif.: Ten Speed Press, 1982.

GRADUATE-SCHOOL PREPARATION

How to Prepare for the GRE (also for MCAT, LSAT, GMAT)
New York: Harcourt, Brace, Jovanovich, 1982.
How to Prepare for the GRE (also for MCAT, LSAT, GMAT, DAT)
Woodbury, N.Y.: Barron's Educational Series, 1982.
How to Get Into Law School
Strickland, Rennard. New York: Hawthorn Books, 1977.

LOVEJOY'S
College Guide

The *only* book you'll ever need to answer all of your questions about any college or university in the United States.

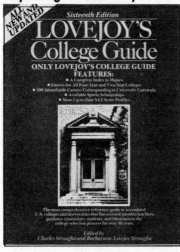

Only *Lovejoy's* includes all of the most up-to-date information on:

■ Financial Aid ■ SAT/ACT Scores Accepted ■ Admission Criteria ■ Major Programs ■ School Ambiance ■ Index to Majors ■ Complete Sports Scholarship Listing ■ Organizations ■ Facilities for Disabled Students ■ Enrollment ■ Student Body Composition ■ 2- and 4-year College Listing ■ Transfer Requirements ■ Graduate Degrees Offered ■ AND MORE!

Sixteenth Edition

$14.95 (paper)   0-671-47170-8
$19.95 (cloth)   0-671-47201-1
576 pages

LOVEJOY'S
GUIDE TO
Graduate Business Schools

The complete reference guide for all potential MBA students, including information on the admissions process and student life.

Complete listings of all accredited Graduate Business Schools with vital information presented in a clear, easy-to-locate format.

Each entry includes: ■ Tuition ■ GMAT Scores Required ■ Student/Faculty Ratios ■ Programs Offered ■ Financial Aid ■ Housing ■ AND MORE!

$14.95 (paper)   272 pages   0-671-44884-6

For your convenience, send check and order to Reader Service, 1230 Avenue of the Americas, NY, NY 10020 *or* call (212) 245-6400, x1182 and charge your order on MasterCard or VISA ($10.00 minimum order). Also available at your local bookstore.

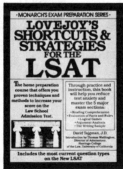